Music

Polity's *Why It Matters* series

In these short and lively books, world-leading thinkers make the case for the importance of their subjects and aim to inspire a new generation of students.

Nicholas Cook

———————

Music

Why It Matters

polity

First published in 2023 by Polity Press

Polity Press
65 Bridge Street
Cambridge CB2 1UR, UK

Polity Press
111 River Street
Hoboken, NJ 07030, USA

ISBN-13: 978-1-5095-4239-0
ISBN-13: 978-1-5095-4240-6(pb)

A catalogue record for this book is available from the British Library.

Library of Congress Control Number: 2022949693

Typeset in 11 on 15pt Sabon
by Cheshire Typesetting Ltd, Cuddington, Cheshire
Printed and bound in the UK by CPI Group (UK) Ltd, Croydon

For further information on Polity, visit our website: politybooks.com

Contents

Acknowledgements

Many people, including members of my family, helped me with this book; in particular I blame my daughter Chloe, who encouraged me when I first floated the idea of bringing together my work on music and my developing political concerns. (The book's period of gestation began with the Brexit referendum, and it was written during the pandemic.) Sometimes the project struck me as crazy, and I am grateful to those who encouraged me to think it might not be: they range from the audiences at virtual seminars where I presented the material to many others who commented on drafts and/or helped in other ways – in particular Daniel Leech-Wilkinson, D. R. M. Irving, Tomás McAuley, Ariana Phillips-Hutton, and Gabrielle Messeder – as well as my wife Louise, my brother Michael, and my son Christopher. (I said it was a family affair.)

Acknowledgements

I found the comments of the publisher's readers exceptionally helpful; one of them was Lawrence Kramer, and while I don't know who the other two were, I am grateful to all three. I thank Pascal Porcheron of Polity Press – who commissioned the book – and his successor Ian Malcolm, both of whom provided valuable guidance on developing it; also Ellen MacDonald-Kramer, who made the process of production as trouble-free (at least for me) as such things can ever be, and Tim Clark, my deft but unintrusive copy editor. Finally I thank the British Academy and the Wolfson Foundation for a research professorship that gave me the time to research and write my forthcoming book *Music, Encounter, Togetherness* (Oxford University Press), in which some of the ideas drawn on in this book are developed in much greater detail.

Or Maybe It Doesn't?

You could say that music matters because it doesn't matter. You don't want to be engaged with weighty issues all the time. Sometimes you need space to relax, to switch off, to contemplate anything and everything and nothing in particular. Or you might want to be taken out of yourself, to socialise, to take music's energy into your body in the half anonymous, half intimate context of clubbing. Or for an hour or two you might leave this world for a better one, a world where beauty or spirituality is all that matters (Figure 1). Music, thought of in many cultures as giving access to some higher state of being, can help with all these things. Above all it is a source of pleasure. These things matter, but you really don't need a book to tell you that.

And actually the idea that music matters because it doesn't matter has a long history, though it's

Figure 1. Fernand Khnopff, *Listening to Schumann* (1883). Royal Museums of Fine Arts of Belgium

not usually expressed quite like that; it's a basic principle of traditional Western music aesthetics. (A health warning: the term 'Western' conflates history, geography, culture, and power, and gives rise to the negative characterisation of the rest of the world as 'non-Western', but the problem is more with the world than the word.) The idea of music's autonomy holds that music has an infinite diversity of potential meaning that transcends the 'real' world: it is a world of its own. In this view music is not 'about' the real world, it is only about itself. This idea was specifically associated with the elite musical culture of the nineteenth and twentieth centuries, what we call Western classical music. Even now it colours some people's thinking about music more generally. And it can very easily slide into the belief that music is nice but doesn't much matter.

I don't buy that. In fact one aim of this short book is to dispose of this kind of thinking once and for all. I do this by picking out a series of areas in which music proves itself to be very much part of the real world. Its more direct effects range from the beneficial – its creation of communal feeling or its contribution to health and welfare – to the harmful, for example its use in warfare. At the same time music is a key arena in which major social issues such as race are played out. Its powers of subliminal persuasion turn it into a political tool, but also create a perspective from which to think about ways in which contemporary politicians mobilise nostalgia and fantasy, as much in their own interests as those of the people whose interests they supposedly serve. (My examples here are mainly drawn from right-wing politicians in contemporary Britain, but similar things are happening in many other countries – and the right does not have a monopoly on such abuses.) Music also throws into relief some problematic dimensions of modern administered society, while in the act of performance it creates social structures that can act as a yardstick against which to measure the still dominant neoliberal culture of hyperindividualism and greed. The Covid-19 pandemic shone an unprecedentedly harsh light on this culture, and I look at some of the new ways people found to use music during the lockdowns, as well as the potential they offer for thinking about music in new ways.

Near the end of the book I come back more explicitly to the question of whether – and if so how and why – music matters. You can make up your own mind at that point.

Music for Good or Ill

Humans are always ready to divide things into opposed categories, which is a problem because in general the world doesn't work like that. So we have 'Western' vs 'non-Western' music (what Stuart Hall called the 'West and the rest' model), we have 'art' vs 'popular' music and so on. There's also a division that arose out of the aesthetics of autonomy: between 'aesthetic' or 'autonomous' music on the one hand (traditionally referred to simply as 'music') and 'applied' music on the other – music the point of which is to do things like make your unborn baby smarter or improve milk yields (I'm speaking of cows). People don't talk much about this distinction, but it is built into everyday life. On the one hand there's concert and recorded music played by professionals, where aesthetic quality is all-important. On the other there's the music without

5

which no royal (or other) wedding or funeral would be complete, or the canned music played in failing restaurants to make them seem less empty, or the music that drives aerobics classes, or that used or created by therapists to help people work through their mental or behavioural problems – all areas in which aesthetic quality is just part of a broader concern for music's contribution to quality of life.

Today's musical pluralism reflects a history of migration and globalisation, coupled to the massive diversification of modes of musical production and consumption resulting from digital sound technology. Many of the old categories and divisions are no longer useful or meaningful. And other social changes have added to this. For example, during most of the twentieth century, music therapy was a specialist practice primarily located in hospitals, but by the end of the century – as with other aspects of care – it had been largely relocated to community settings. There it has become closely linked with the developing practices of community music, as part of a new, emerging area called 'music, health, and wellbeing'. You might see this as demonstrating the increased importance within today's society of 'applied' music, but we don't need to think of it as an either/or. There is rather a continuum of highly diversified musical activity. I maintain that the personal and social dimensions of music are there in the concert hall, and the values of expressive sound in the community music centre or therapy room. The balance may vary, but all music is both 'aesthetic' and 'applied'.

Changing personal and social uses of music have – or should have – a knock-on effect on the study of music, and in this book I touch on that too. Just to set the scene, musicology (a term which in America has the narrower meaning of music history) came into being in the nineteenth century as part of the broader cultural and political phenomenon of nationalism: the very idea of nationhood implied the existence of national cultures that could be traced as far back as possible into the past. Historical traditions of music that originally had nothing to do with one another were amalgamated into national cultures and consolidated in multi-volume editions with titles such as *Denkmäler deutscher Tonkunst* (Monuments of German musical art, published between 1892 and 1931).

Other approaches to the study of music developed around this. Music theorists formulated models of how music worked, whether in terms of national styles, specific composers' styles, or individual compositions. What was called comparative musicology focused on the relationship between Western and – recalling that health warning – non-Western musics, often demonstrating the supposedly exceptional nature of Western music as compared to other traditions seen as inferior. This tied in with the broader historical and cultural ideologies of colonialism and imperialism. Following the partial collapse of European colonialism in the wake of the 1939–45 war, comparative musicology gave way to a new discipline: ethnomusicology, which aims to understand the musics of other cultures on their own terms – an approach sometimes linked with ongoing processes of decolonisation. Popular music studies developed later in the century, initially within literary and cultural studies, but – as the elitist edge of traditional musicology softened – increasingly as a core element of music studies (an umbrella term that I like because it avoids making unproductive distinctions between its constituent disciplines).

Music, health, and wellbeing has not as yet consolidated into an academic field, and people studying it are as likely to be found in departments or divisions of sociology, psychology, or medicine as of music. People who work in this area tend to be well informed about musicology – many of them have music degrees – but not many musicologists know much about music, health, and wellbeing. I think it would be better if they did, and that to get a balanced sense of why music matters you need to think across the whole spectrum of music making. To begin to redress the balance, then, I offer a brief overview of music oriented towards the achievement of broadly social goals.

I turn on the radio at random and hear how the regular beat found in musics across the world helps people with Parkinson's disease to walk, makes it easier for people to articulate feelings they cannot express in words, creates a sense of unity within groups, and even predisposes people to like one another. The social significance and benefits of music have been recognised by multiple governmental and other public groups. The UK Department of Education's 2011 policy paper *The Importance of Music* spoke of its effects on 'self reliance, confidence, self-esteem, sense of achievement and ability to relate to others',[1] and there is an extensive research literature to back this up. Yet in 2020 an article by Colin Harris reported that over the previous five years music teaching in state schools had declined by 21 per cent, and that 'a fifth of all schools in the state sector had no music provision at all'; private schools, by contrast, had increased their music provision by 7 per cent.[2]

That tells us two things. First, music – and culture more generally – is increasingly undervalued by comparison with literacy, numeracy, and subjects seen as directly enhancing employability and economic growth. (British governments have never fully recognised the scale of the employment and overseas earnings generated by music.) And second, music – especially classical music – is increasingly becoming an enclave of the socially privileged. Outside the government-funded education sector, however, the picture is less bleak. A wide range of not-for-profit initiatives focus on music's potential for both personal and social development in contexts that range from institutions (for example prisons) to the wider community. The British Lung Foundation, for example, advocates the health benefits of choral singing, while any number of local programmes target specific communities. London's Wigmore Hall runs 'Music for Life' and 'Singing with Friends' programmes for people with dementia. And it is said that there are more community choirs in the UK than there are fish-and-chip shops.

Music therapy is one of the most longstanding and solidly researched areas of music for health and wellbeing. Its move out of hospitals and into the community was part of a larger move away from medicalised approaches to health – approaches that effectively treated people as bundles of symptoms – and towards a more socialised approach based on

Figure 2. Client and therapist at the Cornwall Music Service Trust, Truro. Credit: Cornwall Music Service Trust

a broader conception of care. The 'music, health and wellbeing' label reflects a concern for wellness, for living well, for flourishing; health becomes a positive concept rather than just meaning absence of illness. Music therapy offers what social psychologist of music Tia DeNora calls 'asylum',[3] referring not to a physical space but rather to a safe, protected environment that facilitates both personal and social rehabilitation. Therapists and clients interact musically, and this fosters communication and empathy, the capacity to see yourself through others' eyes and hear yourself through others' ears (Figure 2). There is a substantial psychological

literature that demonstrates the link between music
and empathy; a study in which DeNora collabo-
rated with musicologists/psychologists Eric Clarke
and Jonna Vuoskoski provided what the authors
called 'narrow but hard-nosed evidence' that hearing music from another culture increases people's
empathy for that culture – even when they are just
listening to a recording.[4] And the belief that 'music
creates empathy, builds connection and gives hope'
underlies the work of Musicians without Borders,
an international organisation that uses music for
peace-building and social change in vulnerable communities from El Salvador to Rwanda, and from
Northern Ireland to Palestine.

Perhaps the highest-profile musical contribution to peace-building is the West-Eastern Divan
Orchestra (WEDO), founded in 1999 by postcolonial theorist Edward Said and pianist and conductor
Daniel Barenboim. It is a youth orchestra predominantly made up of Israeli and Arab musicians, and
the rationale behind it is that, as Barenboim put
it, 'an orchestra requires musicians to listen to one
another':[5] close, reciprocal listening encourages the
mutual understanding and respect that are precon-
ditions for reconciliation. This idea, coupled with
the orchestra's musical quality and appearances
at high-profile venues around the world, attracted

enormous media attention. Reading the reports you might think that music is a silver bullet for solving the world's problems. Of course it isn't; some WEDO students have seen it as a ticket to emigrate to America, and it might be said that by sucking up money and media attention WEDO has hampered more local and sustainable initiatives. Music can help, but it is no substitute for redressing substantive grievances.

(Ethno)musicologist Geoffrey Baker has voiced similar reservations about the Simón Bolívar Symphony Orchestra in Venezuela (which under its former conductor Gustavo Dudamel achieved a comparable profile). Baker complains that media hype has created an atmosphere of 'relentless optimism' in which questioning music's potential for social good is seen as almost heretical.[6] But thinking music is inherently good is a bit like thinking cars are inherently good. Cars enable people who live in rural areas where there is no public transport to get to the shops or to work, help them explore the local countryside, and allow emergency workers to reach accident or crime scenes quickly. But they also run people over, clog up cities, and contribute to climate change. It's the same with music. Music is not intrinsically good or bad. Rather it enhances people's ability to do good or bad, and there is a charge sheet to be faced. Music binds people into a group – think of the drum and fife bands of Northern Ireland – and in so doing unites them against other people, fomenting hatred between classes, ethnicities, or opposing political groups. It can also be used by one group to denigrate others: the 'Turkish' music of eighteenth-century composers such as Mozart broke the rules of 'civilised' (i.e. Western) music and hence represented Hungarians, Turks, and assorted oriental others as deficient. Today, too, music serves to spread anti-Islamic messages; 'Fuck Islam', the title of a song by the Los Angeles-based oi! band Para Elite, tells you all you need to know. Incidentally the band's name is taken from an American-made semi-automatic pistol.

Music's ability to do harm goes beyond spreading messages. Radical political organisations use music as a tool for recruitment. Anders Breivik listened to Clint Mansell's 'Lux Aeterna' as he drove to the youth camp where he killed sixty-nine teenagers in 2011 (he had previously written that 'Lux Aeterna' 'is very inspiring and invokes a type of passionate rage within you'[7]), and may have been listening to it as he gunned them down. In 2006 American musicologist Suzanne Cusick lifted the lid on the use of music for purposes of torture at Guantánamo Bay and elsewhere in the course of the 'war on terror' prompted by 9/11. This practice was based on military research showing that, in Cusick's words, 'sensory overload could be an extremely quick way of breaking down a human being's psychological ability to orient him- or herself in reality, distinguish the hallucinatory from the real, or resist interrogation'; played incessantly, loud music (especially death metal and related genres) is a highly effective means of achieving this objective.[8] In short, music was a key element in a multi-media environment designed to humiliate and dehumanise potential informants, so inducing them to give up hope. And it worked.

Ideology in Disguise

The old idea of aesthetic autonomy claimed that music was in some way 'above' worldly affairs, in particular politics. However during the 1980s and '90s a reforming group of mainly American musicologists – the 'New' musicologists, whose aim was to broaden the scope of their discipline – argued that the very idea of music being above politics was a form of ideological deception. By this they meant that in reality music is an instrument of power – and all the more effective when its role in the exercise of power is concealed.

In the patriarchal society of eighteenth- and nineteenth-century Europe, music reflected and enacted male hegemony. Upper-class women might play the harpsichord or, later, piano (this was an important social accomplishment for Jane Austen heroines hoping to attract a rich husband), so reproducing the work of male composers. The composers were male because the ideology of the day held that women didn't have the same creative powers as men; that is why most of the published works of Fanny Mendelssohn, by any standards a talented composer, appeared under her brother Felix's name. This was seen as the natural order of things. It was like politics in interwar Germany, where the conservative faction claimed to be 'non-political': 'politics' meant the left interfering in the natural order of things, and in this way the conservative status quo was naturalised as just the way the world is. And such thinking isn't limited to Germany. In the UK the Conservative Party long deployed the same tactic, representing itself as the natural party of government. For musicologist Daniel Leech-Wilkinson the status quo encompasses both politics and music: 'classical music performs the right in culture', he says – and then adds, 'in the most beautiful and engaging ways'.[1] Far from being above worldly matters, music acts here as a vehicle of political or ideological deception.

Classical music imperceptibly conveys a historically grounded, Western, white framing of the world as just the way things are. Intentionally or otherwise, it brings with it specifically Western assumptions about what music is, what it is for, the behaviour appropriate to it, and the nature of beauty or value. (That is not to say that, in time, classical music cannot acquire new social meanings. The obvious example is the Chinese culture of classical music performance: a century after their first introduction, Mozart, Beethoven, and the rest have been absorbed into the social fabric of contemporary China.) Much the same might be said of the commercial 'world music' based on Western popular-music norms of rhythm, harmony, and texture; its often stereotyped non-Western elements (instruments, vocalisation, and so forth) end up as decorative features fitted into a white framework. It is not just for economic reasons that it has been seen as a form of colonialism by other means.

And it's not just music. In recent years the right on both sides of the Atlantic has politicised architecture, valorising styles that are represented as 'timeless' and even 'universal' – generally styles that evoke the classical tradition long associated with the display of power. In the US, Donald Trump's 'Making Federal Buildings Beautiful Again' order mandated a return to the neoclassical style exemplified, for example, by the White House. In the UK there was the 'Building Better, Building Beautiful' campaign, chaired by philosopher (Sir) Roger Scruton, known for his writings on the aesthetics of classical architecture and music as well as his vitriolic attacks on the likes of Frank Gehry, Richard Rogers, and Norman Foster (as well as on Nirvana, R.E.M., and the Pet Shop Boys). Ideas of female beauty are equally politicised. There is room in global capitalism for exotic others such as Naomi Campbell, but – by being others – they confirm the norm that beautiful means white; writer and diversity consultant Robin DiAngelo refers to the overwhelming number of white people on lists of the 'Most Beautiful', and cites a *Daily Mail* article entitled 'What would a scientifically perfect face look like?' that appeared alongside the image of a blonde, blue-eyed woman.[2] As with other forms of aestheticisation, beauty is social construct, yet is thought of as something natural, a given. That – as DiAngelo also notes – is why mainstream cosmetic ranges were designed primarily for white skins, until 2017, when Rihanna introduced her Fenty product line.[3]

But what makes music perhaps uniquely effective as ideology is what might be called its double nature. On the one hand it is, obviously, a human artefact, something that people make and that calls on a range of culture-specific social practices and technologies. But at the same time we experience music as if it were a natural language that we know without ever having learned it, and this ability to naturalise is a key source of music's power to persuade. Music presents itself as just what it is. Until the age of recording there was virtually no way of knowing how music had sounded in the past. People looked at centuries-old scores and imagined their sound based on current instruments and performing practices. Only after 1900, as recordings accumulated, did it become evident that in reality performances of 'the same' music have varied wildly from one time (and place) to another. Yet even when faced with unassailable evidence of this, many musicians have continued to resist the idea that music can change so much, with its implication that we know much less than we thought we did about our own musical heritage. Old recordings have defamiliarised the musical past, making our grip on it less secure.

In short, music's present erases its past. It creates the illusion of having always been as it is, and extends that illusion to the cultural practices associated with it. National anthems create and reinforce a sense of unchanging national identity. So do folksongs supposedly handed down from an immemorial past (I'll be coming back to that). These are examples of a widespread phenomenon – the invention of tradition as a means of constructing identity. The monumental editions of national music that I mentioned earlier illustrate this. You can also see it in the ritualised performance of flag-waving Englishness at the Last Night of the Proms, which features such items as 'Rule Britannia', the jingoistic lyrics of which boast of British naval supremacy (the song dates from 1740, when there was more to wave flags about). The Last Night of the Proms goes back only to 1954, yet the fury that greets any attempt to change its format shows how it too is thought of as embodying a timeless Englishness. It contributes to the construction and maintenance of national identity under the guise of merely celebrating it.

The mechanism behind music's powers of persuasion – in this case through naturalising the status quo and so creating a sense of innate nationhood – is most clearly seen in advertising music. An example I like to cite is an old TV commercial for the Prudential insurance company, where (among other things) both harmony and melody are targeted at the point where the Prudential logo appears.[4] Musically the commercial is designed to lead to that point, meaning that the logo appears with the force of apparent inevitability. The musical process is mapped onto the words and images, which stress the importance of choosing a pension plan while you are still young. They set out the problem to which Prudential is the solution. But the logic that drives this – the proof as it were – is all in the music. Musicologist James Garratt describes the same process at work in a campaign ad Bernie Sanders used when running for the 2016 Democratic nomination: it is 'carefully calculated to press the right affective buttons; the visuals are cut to fit the beat of the song, crescendoing into the climactic refrain "They've all come to look for America"'.[5] In such ways music can control or choreograph your attention, highlight certain things while de-emphasising others. And in doing this, whether it concerns Prudential pension plans or the Democratic nomination, music can affirm the rightness of the message. It makes no difference whether the message is actually true or not.

Discussions of music can smuggle political implications into apparently non-political discourse. The novelist and travel writer Beverley Nichols published a book entitled *Verdict on India* in 1944, three years before the end of British rule. Among other things it set out an argument that probably seemed self-evident to many of his readers. The improvised nature of Indian music, Nichols said, illustrates how Indians lack the application and self-discipline necessary to bring the work of creating music to its conclusion.[6] The implication was clear: such indolence, or frivolity, demonstrated that Indians were not ready for self-rule. Nichols was measuring Indian music against the Western norm by which (as he says) Chopin may have improvised, thinking of George Sand, but only until he got out his pen and started on the serious business of writing music. The Indians never got out their pens, and that is why there has never been an Indian Beethoven. As with the eighteenth-century 'Turkish' music, the racialised other fails to conform to Western norms and must therefore be deficient. You can see the problem with the logic when it is explained (it's the 'therefore'). But the point is that with music you don't have to explain it.

Music, Race, Empire

It isn't hard to identify the racial assumptions built into an imperialist mindset such as Nichols's, and music is a key arena where culture and race intersect. What I referred to as 'Western popular music' has its origins in an amalgam of musical styles drawn from a diversity of African cultures, fused into a distinctively Black musical language in the American plantations and later in urban centres: there it not only hybridised with vernacular traditions of white music but also was drawn into an emerging politics of race. Central to this was blackface, the most popular form of mass culture in nineteenth-century America, where white Americans 'blacked up' and impersonated Black people (Figure 3), denigrating them while perhaps at the same time expressing a sly envy of them. As the musicologist Matthew Morrison says, 'masked performance developed

Figure 3. Actress Ira Donnette in blackface, 1909.
J. Willis Sayre Collection of Theatrical Photographs,
University of Washington Libraries

sonic and bodily "markings", or scripts, that became closely attached to stereotyped ideas of race', and at the same time 'a space for whiteness was constructed and freely articulated through the blackface mask'.[1] This gave rise on the one hand to a cast of essentialised racial types that encoded otherness (Figure 4), and on the other to a heightened

Figure 4. Zip Coon (music cover from 1834). Library of Congress

sense of racialised whiteness. Blackface naturalised the racial binary, as if Black people really were the way white performers represented them, and built it into American popular music. Black musicians who wanted to achieve commercial success had to conform to white understandings of authentic Blackness – that is, to the stereotypes that white Americans had created. Racial inequity can take convoluted forms.

But it's not just popular music. Race is a dimension of Western classical music too. Black classical musicians are relatively few in number, whether for reasons of colour, class, or economic circumstance; until 2015, when Chi-chi Nwanoku founded the Chineke! Orchestra, there was no professional orchestra in Europe with a majority of Black and ethnically diverse members. However, there have always been Black individuals who excelled at classical music. The music of the British mixed-race composer and conductor Samuel Coleridge-Taylor – whose success made even (Sir) Edward Elgar jealous, but who died in 1912 at the age of thirty-seven – originally bore no traces of his Sierra Leonean heritage. But he was taken up in African American circles and became increasingly engaged with African culture. He brought both African American and West African elements into his compositions (though the overall style remained what might be called classical modern). Equally significant was his engagement with Black politics in America: he corresponded with such major figures as Booker Washington and W. E. B. Du Bois. Perhaps most telling, however, was a small incident from his early career when he was rehearsing a mainly female string orchestra at the Croydon Conservatoire of Music. Someone referred to him as 'black' – at that time a slightly impolite term – and 'one of the girls retorted indignantly, "Please don't call Mr Coleridge-Taylor black; he is only black outside".'[2] In the 1920s Germans similarly referred to Black classical musicians as 'Negroes with white souls' – the exceptions that proved the rule of white musical supremacy.[3]

Like sport, classical music today sees itself as a colourblind meritocracy. Even the most successful Black musicians, however, have another tale to tell. When in 1999 the opera singer Willard White appeared on the long-running BBC radio programme *Desert Island Discs* (in which 'castaways' choose the recordings they would like to have if stranded on a desert island), the presenter, Sue Lawley, raised the subject of racial discrimination and was shocked when White spoke of it in the world of opera: 'but I'm amazed that you say it's at work in the world of opera', Lawley expostulated. 'I find that very difficult to believe.' White replied, 'Don't get me on a track where I can say "well, you're not Black". You don't know. Whether you find it difficult to believe or not, it's there. And that's it.'[4]

Another example of racism in classical music is attitudes to East Asian performers, of whom there are many (not surprisingly, as East Asia has become the heartland of Western classical music in the twenty-first century). Since at least the 1930s the idea has circulated that Asian performers may have daunting technical skills, but lack cultural understanding of Western music and consequently cannot play with genuine expressiveness. Asian American musicologist Mari Yoshihara speaks of a concert at Livingstone, New Jersey, that the Japanese-born but American-resident pianist Makiko Hirata gave in 1999. A review expressed astonishment that a Japanese pianist could play Chopin so well: 'Miss Hirata was working with something that would be as "foreign" to us as if we were trying to play Japanese music.'[5] In reality there are many Asian pianists who are far more familiar with Chopin than with 'their own' music; Hirata herself holds a doctorate in piano performance from Rice University in Houston, Texas. But the critic doesn't ask about Hirata's background or training, apparently believing that ethnicity is all that counts. I detect no hint of hostility in the review – and yet it reveals a pattern of thought that is inherently racist. Similar prejudices take an uglier form in relation to the innumerable prodigy videos on YouTube, a very high proportion of which are by Asian children (and often playing Chopin). They frequently attract such comments from anglophone viewers as 'I bet if she messed up on a note she would've been beaten to death.'[6]

The study of music and race was part of the expanded agenda of the 'New' musicology, and another term used to describe such work was 'critical musicology'. Here 'critical' is to be understood in the sense of Frankfurt-style critical theory: the aim was to bring to light the signs of hegemony and prejudice buried within music from the past. It began in the 1980s with gender critique, which showed how the supposedly autonomous – non-political – music of the Western 'art' tradition in fact reflected the patriarchal assumptions embedded in Western society more generally. Actually it would be odd if it didn't, and the purpose of the critique was in part to overthrow the ideology of musical autonomy. But sometimes a case could be made that music in some way subverted dominant gender structures and so became a vehicle for progressive social change. More recent examples might be the messages of women's empowerment spread by such artists as Madonna, the Spice Girls, and Beyoncé.

Race critique in music follows a similar pattern but was also influenced by postcolonial theory – an

30

approach that had developed primarily in literary studies (with Edward Said at its head). In relation to music it took two main forms, one of which I have already touched on: critical readings of the classical repertory, showing how composers had evoked the music of others – particularly Islamic others – in such a way as to represent them as defective, clumsy, unskilful, or barbaric. (There were also traces of humour and perhaps again envy in the music, but musicologists tended to be less sensitive to these.) Similarly, eighteenth- and nineteenth-century operas created an image of the orient as populated by wicked and/or self-indulgent pashas, harems, and slave boys that emphasised the otherness of eastern cultures, their non-conformity to the basic values that define the West. Much the same has been said of the late twentieth- and twenty-first-century operas of John Adams and Peter Sellars.[7]

The other and more recent form of postcolonial critique is historical analysis of how, ever since the sixteenth century, music has served as an instrument of colonisation and empire. Because of its naturalising qualities, the introduction of Western music to colonies – often in the context of religious conversion – was an effective vehicle of culture change, subliminally or otherwise altering subaltern perceptions of the world and their place in it. Western music was seen as scientifically advanced, like Western technology and medicine, and so contributing to modernisation – a process presented as natural, inevitable, and positive, but in reality serving the interests of colonial exploitation. (Modernisation was also a strategy for nation building by formerly colonised, or never colonised, countries: that is how Western music came to play a leading role in Japan and China.)

As (ethno)musicologist D. R. M. Irving argues, two linked qualities attributed to Western music were particularly important for its imperialist role: exceptionalism and universalism.[8] Exceptionalism is the doctrine that Western civilisation is fundamentally different from, and superior to, all other cultures. Western rationality – the core value of the European Enlightenment – was seen as the fundamental justification for colonial and imperial expansion: it lay at the heart of Western claims to be bringing civilisation to the colonised world. In the same way, Western music was seen as exceptional, its rational basis ensuring its superiority to other musical traditions. The proof was supposed to be the Western invention of that most scientific of musical principles, the combination of individual parts to create harmony, and with it the sense of music moving purposefully towards a goal. This explains the controversy and anxious debate that resulted when in the 1770s the navigator James Cook – Captain Cook – brought back reports of Tongan islanders singing in parts.

And exceptionalism was linked to universalism. Because Western music was exceptional, and because of its uniquely scientific basis, it was seen as having a universal value that other musics lacked. The common idea of music as a 'universal language' looks like an optimistic spin on music's ability to communicate directly across cultural boundaries in a way that linguistic media cannot (and there is more than a grain of truth in this, depending on what you mean by 'communicate'). But when people talk about music as a universal language they more often than not mean *Western* music, and in that context it becomes a very different kind of claim. The postcolonial theorist Homi Bhabha has written that 'universalism ... masks ethnocentric norms, values, and interests'.[9] Seen that way, it wasn't just for failing to conform to Western norms that Nichols was censuring the Indians: it was for failing to conform to the universal standards of civilisation.

But as I said earlier, just as music is never simply good, so it is never simply bad. As in the case of gender, so in colonial contexts it could be a progressive force. It created contact zones, such as the nautches of late eighteenth-century India in which coloniser and colonised could share an enjoyment of music and dance. There is a genre known as the 'Hindostannie air', based on sessions where Indian musicians performed songs, and musicians with a Western background tried to recreate them in a form intelligible to European ears; the results were then performed in colonial circles. In the surviving notations you can sometimes see the Western musicians sacrificing basic, supposedly universal principles of European music – 'their' music – in the attempt to create a bridge between cultures. And such examples add light and shade to images of imperial hegemony drawn solely in black and white. In such contexts a form of cross-cultural intimacy could develop: ethnomusicologist Katherine Schofield speaks of 'a two-way affair of mutual curiosity and delight in musical minutiae – an open exploration of affinities and possibilities through trained bodily proficiencies, rather than a closing of ears to offensive differences'.[10]

Music can also act as a focus of resistance to hegemony. In 1930s China, for example, massed choral singing became a key means through which military resistance against Japanese attempts to colonise China was mobilised. And for Australian singer-songwriter Nick Cave, songs are 'dangerous little bombs of truth'[11] – an apt characterisation for Country Joe and the Fish's 'The Fish Cheer' (1967), which spread like an internet meme across America and catalysed resistance to the Vietnam war. In all these ways music has not just reflected the history of empire, but been an integral part of it.

2020 and After

Although postcolonial theory and decolonisation studies blur into one another, there is a difference of emphasis: both are strongly informed by politics and ethics, but while postcolonial theory is an essentially historical field of study, decolonisation studies focus on ways in which colonial values persist in the supposedly postcolonial world. Global corporations and multinational institutions such as the International Monetary Fund (IMF) are examples, and so is the continuing discrimination, in Western societies as elsewhere, against minority groups, even within legislative frameworks supposed to prevent it. Race is just one dimension of such discrimination, but as I write this – two years on from the killing in May 2020 of rapper and freestyle improviser George Floyd, the 'prolonged and full-throated, visceral outpouring of rage' that followed it,[1] and the Black Lives Matter protests that continued throughout that summer and beyond – it is hard not to see it as the central one.

Musicologists responded with studies of music's role in abetting or pushing back against racism. In the more inclusive field of sound studies there was research into American police killings, using a variety of sonic sources to understand the dynamics and significance of such events.[2] More generally the effect was to push racial and other forms of social inequity up the agenda of music studies. In an editorial published in late 2020 in *Acta Musicologica* (the journal of the International Musicological Society), Philip Bohlman and Federico Celestini spoke of the events of that year as 'a moment of recognition to which musicology must respond';[3] they advocated studies of music's complicity in engrained inequities, together with a rethinking of the structures of music research and teaching in light of it. And while this move towards a more socially engaged or 'applied' musicology originated in North America, it spread to other parts of the anglophone world, and beyond, at the speed of optical fibre.

This development was part of a larger, cross-disciplinary movement to bring into the open the racist assumptions and values built into mainstream discourses, and it has become a major route through which politics enters the academy; music can hardly be separated from the discourses around it, and this is a significant dimension of how music matters today. I was involved on the fringes of one controversy over music and race, and will take that as my example. As far as I was concerned the story started in 2019, when I received an invitation from a small American academic journal (the *Journal of Schenkerian Studies*) to respond to some criticisms of my 2007 book *The Schenker Project: Culture, Race, and Music Theory in Fin-de-siècle Vienna*. The criticisms were contained in a keynote address to the (American) Society for Music Theory delivered by the theorist Philip Ewell, a video of which was available on the web. But first I need to explain what was at issue.

Heinrich Schenker (1868–1935) was a musician, critic, and educator who developed an original way of thinking about the canonical works of the German musical tradition from Bach to Brahms. Without going into unnecessary detail, he interpreted them as elaborately hierarchical structures (think Russian dolls); for him this was the underlying principle of the great German masterworks – what made them exceptional, qualitatively different from other music. And he believed that later musicians had lost sight of this as part of a general cultural decline that he aimed to reverse. Schenker was himself Jewish, as were many of his pupils, and following Hitler's rise to power several of them emigrated to America. The result was that in the years after 1945 Schenker's approach became established in key American universities and conservatories as the leading approach to analysing – explaining the inner workings of – Western classical music. In translating the theory from interwar Austria to postwar America, however, Schenkerian scholars suppressed aspects of Schenker's writings that would not play well in America, in particular his highly reactionary politics, extreme German nationalism, and metaphysical speculations. They published sanitised translations in which such passages were toned down, explained away in footnotes, or simply left out.

Towards the end of the century there was a strong reaction against such practices within the Schenkerian community, and modern translations are unexpurgated. There was also debate about the ethics of deploying an analytical approach that has historical roots in German nationalism and right-wing extremism. The generally agreed position (which I took in *The Schenker Project*) is that you can use the theory but should never forget where it came from. In retrospect I don't think this cuts it. 'I must confess', the eminent Schenkerian theorist Carl Schachter has written, 'that I never think about Schenker's politics, religion, or philosophy when engaged in analyzing a piece or refining a theoretical concept, and I very rarely discuss these matters when teaching analysis'.[4] Put differently, he forgets about the theory's origins whenever he actually uses it.

My book argued that to understand why Schenker's theory is as it is – and why it changed as it did when it arrived in America – you have to understand it in context. For example, I argued that important aspects of Schenker's theory were conditioned by his Jewish heritage. The basic idea is that you look *through* the surface of music (the outermost dolls, so to speak) to the structure that is concealed within it and gives the music its aesthetic power and vitality – and this resonates with the traditional Jewish trope of searching for the truth that lies behind appearances. That is in turn linked to the long history of Jewish persecution, which for Schenker meant the concealment of his Jewish identity and faith within a city that during his lifetime was a hotbed of antisemitism. (This is why my book's subtitle includes the word 'race'.) So I was surprised to find that Ewell's principal criticism was that Schenkerian theorists (of which he cited

me as one) believe that issues of race have nothing
to do with music theory. Ewell, however, was not
concerned with Schenker's own ethnicity. His argument was rather that Schenker was an anti-Black
racist, and that his theory – indeed music theory in
general – is itself inherently racist.

I don't know whether Schenker, who died in
1935, had any personal dealings with Black people.
But there is plenty of evidence for his racist views.
In my book I spoke of the 'grisly exhibits in the
Schenkerian chamber of horrors', including a
few casual but extraordinarily offensive – by any
standards racist – remarks about Black people,
in particular the Senegalese troops placed in the
occupied Saarland by the League of Nations in the
aftermath of the 1914–18 war: in 1921 Schenker
referred to 'the ignominy of its black troops – the
advance party of its genitalitis, of the flesh of its
flesh, of the cannibal spirit of its spirit'.[5] Schenker's
publications during and after the First World War
contain extensive passages of almost unhinged
vituperation against the Allied powers; in 1916, for
example, he described the English as 'barbarous,
mendacious, revolting as ever a race that has med-
dled on the earth', and there is plenty more where
that came from.[6] It's worth noting that – typically of
its time and place – Schenker's use of the term 'race'

doesn't have the direct connotation of colour that it does in twenty-first-century America; for him, the English, French, and Italians were all separate races.

As usual, things aren't entirely black and white. A diary entry from 1915 expresses Schenker's sympathy for 2,000 Algerian riflemen who died when a French ship was torpedoed ('the fate of these savages almost moves me more than that of our Europeans. They have been taken from their homeland and are now lost. For whom? Who will ask after them? Who will report their names, learn their fate, avenge them?!').[7] All the same, if Schenker were alive today, his racism would undoubtedly be considered beyond the pale. The Algerian riflemen, after all, are still 'savages', reflecting the standard imperialist mindset of the time – an ugly synthesis of Darwinian evolutionary theory and racial 'science', according to which different races could be placed in a hierarchy, with white Caucasians (or 'Aryans') at the top. However objectionable and intemperately expressed, Schenker's racist views were not untypical of his time and place – unlike his German nationalism, which was so excessive and so xenophobic that it alienated a number of his friends and supporters.

I said that in my response, and also queried the logic through which Ewell linked Schenker's racism and his music theory. In the words of an article published in 2020, he observed that, in Schenker's theory, higher levels of the musical hierarchy 'govern' or 'control' the lower levels, and that in the same way 'Schenker believed that blacks must be governed and controlled by whites'. From this parallel Ewell concluded that 'there exists a strong white-supremacist element to [Schenker's] theories about both race and music in light of his anti-black racism', as a result of which 'this racism has infected and become integral to the white racial frame of music theory'.[8] Ewell did acknowledge that 'the linkage of Schenker's racism with his music theories is necessarily speculative', adding 'this is obviously my interpretation'.[9] All the same, it bothered me that the same kind of argument might be used to show that mathematics is inherently racist: inequality and hierarchy are basic elements of mathematics.[10]

I kept my response short and didn't engage with the broader question of how far present-day music theory is inherently racist; I saw that as an essentially American matter on which it wasn't my business to comment. I emailed my response to the journal editor and thought no more of it until July 2020 – two months after the George Floyd killing – when I was told that the Vice Chancellor of the University of Cambridge (for which I had worked until my retirement three years earlier) had received a letter asking him to take action against me for my 'anti-Semitic rhetoric, anti-Black racism, and apologist rhetoric'. I imagine the reference to 'apologist rhetoric' reflected my saying that Schenker's racism was typical of the imperialist mindset around 1900; I wrote to the author of the letter asking what the 'anti-Semitic rhetoric' and 'anti-Black racism' referred to, but she didn't reply.

I googled and discovered that my response to Ewell's criticisms was just one of fifteen in the *Journal of Schenkerian Studies*,[11] written by a variety of American music theorists. Many of these responses were more expansive than mine. Some insisted that music theory and theorists are colourblind. Others drew a distinction between the murky origins of Schenker's theory and its practice today (especially since the theory has developed a great deal since it arrived in America). A few, like me, had problems with Ewell's parallel between musical and racial control. But several welcomed Ewell's intervention, on the grounds that traditional music theory – and Schenker's in particular – is exclusionary: it reinforces undesirable social values and dogmatically rules out alternative directions in which music theory might develop.

One or two responses were problematic. One was anonymous, so contravening a basic principle of academic publication. Another condemned the ovation Ewell had received after his keynote address as 'outrageous and dangerous', spoke of 'bringing Blacks up to "standard"', and placed Ewell's critique in 'the much larger context of Black-on-Jew attacks in the United States'. That blew the lid. There were open letters from students, scholars, and academic organisations directed against the journal and contributors to it. The university that published the journal suspended its editor and conducted a review of its editorial policies; the matter ended up in the courts. For a few weeks, social media and the blogosphere were full of Schenkergate, as the controversy became known. Taking the anti-woke side, Slipped Disc (Norman Lebrecht's notorious classical music blog) had a field day. Even Fox News ran the story. I had stumbled into cancel culture and the culture wars.

By the time I had read all this, my earlier view that the issue of racism in music theory wasn't my business had come to look hopelessly blinkered. Twentieth-century music theory – essentially the creation and application of models to explain music's meaningfulness – is built on nineteenth-century foundations. So it stands to reason – but had not been acknowledged – that the racist, elitist, and imperialist assumptions of that time were built into its disciplinary frame. If you think about it (which I hadn't), it is pretty obvious that institutionalised music theory is steeped in the very assumptions that made music an instrument of empire. It traditionally assumes that 'music' means Western 'art' music, and aims to explain what many theorists (including Schenker) have seen as the unique and exceptional qualities of that tradition. It seeks to substantiate the rational – even scientific – nature of the music, and in this way underwrites its universality. And in this context the ethical question about deploying an approach that has historical roots in right-wing politics and German nationalism takes on a more tangible form: how far may music theory serve to naturalise the pernicious values that are built into it, most obviously elitism – the belief that some human beings are naturally superior to others, from which racism flows – and the rightness of Western ways of thinking, the sense that they embody how the world is? Never forgetting where the theory came from is an evasion of the issue.

What follows from this? Before I come to that, I need to sketch a larger context for Schenkergate. When the world changes, curricula need to change.

The idea of 'decolonising the curriculum' emerged around 2015 and has spread across academia on both sides of the Atlantic. But it came centre stage in the wake of the George Floyd killing. As with critical theory, the basic demand is to seek out and eliminate traces of hegemonic thinking, or at least to create awareness of its presence. Students at the Cambridge Faculty of Music, for example, drew up an open letter pointing out how Western classical music is made up of works 'deemed "great", "canonic", lying *outside* of historical context', and arguing that 'histories of colonialism, imperialism, racism, white supremacy' should be used to 'at least contextualise many of these works and their authors'.[12] They were not asking 'for western music to be taken off the curriculum', the students explained, rather 'we wish to study it outside a bubble of "soft" white supremacy and liberal imperialism'. These were essentially achievable demands, and curricular changes followed – as evidenced by a story about the Cambridge Faculty that appeared in the right-wing British newspaper *The Daily Telegraph* in May 2022. The headline was 'Decolonise your ears as Mozart's works may be an instrument of Empire, students told'.

In this context Ewell's prescriptions for reforming music theory seemed entirely reasonable: people who work in music theory should be aware of the white racial framing that has historically characterised their field; more attention should be given to musicians of colour, and to the theories either explicitly formulated by them or implicit in their work; music theory should embrace other musical and music-theoretical traditions; and there should be greater emphasis on diversity in the hiring of music theorists. Apart from the final point, these recommendations involve the addition to the curriculum of new elements. As such they prompt the objections that always accompany curricular reform: there isn't room for all this; the changes will dilute the existing curriculum, and undermine the basic skills that students need to acquire; and anyhow we don't have anyone to teach it (that is where Ewell's final point comes in). Such problems are there to be solved. But the Cambridge students also made another point which I think is relevant to Schenkergate: 'when we talk about "diversity"', they said, 'the word usually refers to "adding in" composers and musicians who are not white. The system remains the same'. Changing the content without changing the system can at best be only part of the solution.

The reference to Cambridge brings up a key difference between the American and British perspectives.

In Britain the various elements of music studies – historical musicology, music theory, ethnomusicology, and popular music studies, together with composition and performance – are generally combined within curricula, with a department of music made up of individual specialists in these fields. By contrast, in America faculty and student numbers are generally greater and these elements have greater autonomy: in effect they are discrete, if related, disciplines. In this context 'the system' relates to the disciplinary identity of music theory as, on the one hand, a set of academic practices distinct from those of musicology, ethnomusicology and the rest, and on the other hand an institutional entity that organises programmes of study, administers related budgets, and so forth. It also impacts music theorists' self-identity and career structures: they hold professorships in music theory, publish in music theory journals, and attend Society for Music Theory conferences. All this conditioned the shape that Schenkergate took (and explains my original feeling that it wasn't my business; I don't think of myself as a music theorist in the American sense).

As I said, music theory came into being as a discipline at a time when – and within a social class for which – 'music' meant 'Western "art" music': that is why it is simply called 'music theory'. It is a product of, and through skills training supports, a historically white, elite tradition (though one in which more Black musicians have participated than most people think).[13] It is structured around the specific aesthetic aims and resources of Western 'art' music. Although music theorists today are much more open to issues of culture and history than they were when the discipline came into being, its disciplinary identity lies in the assumption that music can be understood in its own terms, abstracted from social context. In addition it engages with music primarily in its notated form: underlying this is the idea that music can be decomposed into a structure of notes (more on this later) and so, as it were, reverse engineered. It also approaches music as a repertory of enduring works rather than a socially engaged practice. In all these ways it is based on an ontology of music – a conception of what music is – that is specifically Western, and that doesn't adequately represent the multifaceted nature of music as a social phenomenon even within the West. Above all, as I said, it is based on the premise that Western 'art' music is amenable to rational understanding and in that sense scientific. It is this set of premises that marks music theory out from the other disciplines of music studies. And in this way the problem with updating the content of music theory is that it leaves the disciplinary frame – the system – in place.

It has for some time been my impression that American music theory has a mission problem. Theorist Stephen Rings memorably calls it 'a discipline apart, a sort of blissed-out, sylvan glade within the Left melancholic academy'.[14] This is quoted by another American theorist, Bryan Parkhurst, in his review of a book about music and contemporary capitalism. Parkhurst emphasises the importance of the issues the book raises but complains about the author's 'facile comparisons between musical and social structures'. People working on such issues, Parkhurst continues, 'will need at some point to consider the input of those whose vocation it is to engage in . . . "sustained, active nearness to musical materials, sonic and physical" – namely music theorists'.[15] And perhaps, he adds, that 'is what's left . . . for music theorists to do'.

The subtext of Parkhurst's article as I read it is that music theory is increasingly sustained by its institutions (techniques, curricula, academic departments and societies, journals, career structures) rather than by a coherent and defensible academic agenda. It seems to me that, rather than retaining music theory and attempting to decolonise it through curricular reform, it would be better to start at the other end.

That means retaining and building on the many and diverse approaches to achieving 'sustained, active nearness to musical materials, sonic and physical' that music theorists have developed over many years – approaches whose value I am not questioning – and considering how they might be best positioned and mobilised within a more flexible, inclusive, and decentred field of music studies than the disciplinary structure inherited from an imperial past.

And it's not just the disciplines of music studies as traditionally conceived. Increasingly the study of music is extending into a variety of academic fields that contribute to the understanding of music and music making – fields that range from psychology, sociology and anthropology to interdisciplinary performance studies, dance studies, and computer science. In short, re-envisioning music theory for the post-2020 world entails a new norm that cuts across existing disciplinary divisions.[16] After all, the increasing concern of today's music theorists with issues of culture and history demonstrates how the twentieth-century disciplinary order is breaking down. What is still called 'music theory' is changing even as its disciplinary institutions remain stubbornly in place.

But it goes still further. Music studies is just one area in which existing disciplinary structures and the larger programme of decolonisation collide. Australian ethnomusicologists, whether Indigenous or white, struggle to represent traditional models of knowledge production within the epistemological structures of the academy; historians from the Global South critique Western hegemony by deploying Western-style argumentation. International academia is organised around fundamental criteria – of rationally based argumentation, of the transparent marshalling of evidence and the acknowledgement of other researchers – that have a long and distinctively Western history. So isn't the international system of higher education and research, like the system of global capitalism and the IMF, itself an example of the perpetuation of a white, Western frame within a supposedly decolonising world? Can and should there be such things as truly universal academic standards, rather than white-frame standards masquerading as universal? I don't have answers to these questions.

Otegha Uwagba writes that 'it's relatively easy to be a theoretical anti-racist'.[17] In the same way it's relatively easy for a retired, white professor from Cambridge to pontificate about decolonising the curriculum. And in an open letter addressed to 'white UK/US/Europhile music colleagues' and entitled 'Listening is not enough', an international group of scholars engaged with music and race have written that 'white people/we need to shut up, we/white people must stop posturing, pontificating and prescribing as these effectively silence and usurp people of colour's voices'.[18] There's another thing too. One of the best ways of preventing change is by showing how difficult it is, how the sensible thing to do is to put it on hold until there is a better understanding of the issues involved and resources are available to address it properly rather than just papering over the cracks. Does what I've said amount to kicking an intractable problem into the long grass? I hope not, because when curricula change, the world may change too. And it certainly needs to.

Music and Asocial Individualism

After referring to Black Lives Matter, the *Acta Musicologica* editorial I mentioned said that 'among the many reasons that this moment exacts its claim for reckoning, the recognition that racism is and has been systemic is especially important'. As critical race theorists explain, what makes racism such an intractable problem is that it is widely thought of in terms of what Robin DiAngelo calls 'asocial individualism'. Racial attitudes and practices are seen as a matter of individual morality (this is what sociologist and critical race theory pioneer Eduardo Bonilla-Silva calls the 'prejudice approach'). It follows that identifying racist attitudes in yourself is tantamount to branding yourself a bad person.

But in reality, DiAngelo writes, racism is 'a far-reaching system that functions independently from the intentions or self-images of individual actors'.[1]

Speaking of the white racial frame of music theory is not the same as accusing individual music theorists of racism. Racism is invisible to those who are racially privileged, because it is a taken-for-granted part of the social environment; it's like fish not being aware of the water they live in. That is the problem with the still widely accepted and ostensibly reasonable principle of racial colourblindness.[2] Hiring committees claim they are indifferent to applicants' ethnicity and consider only individual merit, as if applicants of different ethnicities were competing on a level playing field. But they aren't, and so those who claim to be colourblind perpetuate systemic inequity while failing to see what they are doing.

What DiAngelo calls 'white fragility' is a defensiveness among the racially privileged that arises from being told you should feel guilt for something you can't even see. The purpose of DiAngelo's book, and of others designed for a predominantly white readership, is to help readers become aware of the systemic nature of racism and their own embeddedness within the system; the aim is to instil not guilt but understanding, the prerequisite for change. In the UK, the Sewell Report into race and ethnic disparities, commissioned by the Conservative government and published in 2021, denied the existence of systemic racism in Britain. The reason for its hostile reception is that this represented a refusal to engage with the problems of race in British society at the only level at which they can be effectively tackled. As illustrated by the long history of scandals in London's Metropolitan Police Service, you do not get rid of racism by identifying a few 'bad apples'.

There are direct links between this and music. Consider white ethnomusicologists who conduct fieldwork with racially underprivileged groups such as the Indigenous peoples of Australia. At one time – and not so long ago – researchers studied such groups in much the same detached, or 'objective', manner that sociobiologists might study the mating behaviour of tree frogs. They might claim to be colourblind, yet they were reducing people to specimens: unconscious racism was built into the research method. Nowadays ethnomusicologists are more likely to seek engagement with the communities they study, collaborating with Indigenous individuals and sometimes presenting or publishing jointly with them. Racial equity informs their way of working. Combining critical race theory and a highly effective story-telling format, Australian ethnomusicologist Elizabeth Mackinlay has recounted the extended process by which she came to understand her own racial privilege and to build this understanding into her professional work.[3] For her this is an essential ethnomusicological skill.

DiAngelo's argument about the systemic nature of race applies to many other areas too. The influential creativity theorist Mihali Csikszentmihalyi has developed what he calls the 'systems' model of creativity (which applies as much to music as to anything else), and by this he means that creative individuals work within, and depend on, social systems. Like racism, creativity is both social and systemic. Just as with racism, seeing creativity as a purely individual matter makes it unintelligible. Yet asocial individualism is everywhere in inherited thinking about Western 'art' music. And it goes beyond people seeing Beethoven's Fifth Symphony as the composer's own exclusive achievement and celebrating his genius.

Around 1800 the Western classical tradition came to be conceived as a repertory of masterworks bequeathed by the great composers and reproduced in performance by musicians committed to realising the masters' intentions in the most faithful way possible; over the last half century this image has gradually faded, but it has not disappeared. It is just part of the nineteenth-century mythologisation of classical music. For example, great composers such as Beethoven were seen as transcending the musical rules to which the merely talented must conform. Again, the geniuses were said to be 'inspired', meaning that entire symphonies came to them in a creative flash, merely needing to be written down. That idea, however, is comprehensively exploded by Beethoven's sketchbooks, which show that he composed in broadly the same way that anybody carries out a complex cognitive task: through planning followed by the roughing out and then refinement of details – a process that in Beethoven's case sometimes went smoothly but could involve false starts, cul-de-sacs, and occasionally tearing things up and starting over (or giving up).

I'm not suggesting that individual talent doesn't play a crucial part in musicianship of any kind. But all composers work within a complex ecology, in Beethoven's time ranging from paper manufacturers and stockists to copyists, piano makers and tuners, performers of their works, amanuenses, and either aristocratic patrons or fee-paying students. And while it may be a stretch to count all of these people as directly implicated in the act of composition, Beethoven worked in creative collaboration with performers who specialised in playing his music – like the Schuppanzigh Quartet, which premiered many of his string quartets, or the orchestras (generally ad hoc ensembles put together for the occasion) with whom he rehearsed his symphonic works until his deafness made it impossible. Beethoven's creativity depended on this ecology as much as tree frogs (of which there are many endangered species) depend on theirs. It is a grotesque distortion of reality to reduce this complex web of social interaction to a 'big I' model of creativity – the artist in the garret whose genius towers above humanity.

But that is exactly the 'Great Man' (*sic*) model of history promulgated in 1840 by the Scottish essayist and historian Thomas Carlyle.[4] According to this, history – whether in the arts or politics – is produced by the great men, the geniuses. That is more or less how Schenker saw music history, but in the context of political history a recent and pertinent example comes from Boris Johnson, still UK Prime Minister when I first drafted this. In 2014 he published a biography of (Sir) Winston Churchill entitled *The Churchill Factor: How One Man Made History*. You don't need to read it: the subtitle says it all, and in case you miss it Johnson repeats it on page 5 ('one man can make all the difference'). The text is littered with references to greatness and genius (Churchill was 'a thorough-going genius' whose father had been 'cheated of the greatness that should have been his'; 'the closer you get to Winston Churchill, the more convinced you become of his genius', and so forth). The book is cast as a rebuttal of what Johnson characterises as the Marxist belief that history is driven by larger forces, leaving no space for great men. While he is concerned to defend Churchill – although 'an imperialist', Churchill 'believed in the greatness of Britain and her civilising mission'[5] – there is also a more personal agenda: Johnson portrays Churchill as the outsider who nevertheless proved to be the only man up to the job when the chips were down. That is essentially how Johnson sold himself to the British electorate in 2019.

Ethnomusicologist Timothy Taylor refers to the nineteenth- and twentieth-century conception of the artist as the clearest embodiment of today's ideology of entrepreneurial individualism[6] – an ideology that is grounded in politics and economics but extends into daily life and people's sense of who they are. Any form of systemic injustice becomes intractable when seen in terms of asocial individualism. First disseminated (though ambivalently) by Alexis de Tocqueville in the mid nineteenth century, its most notorious advocate was the American but Russian-born and stridently anti-communist writer Ayn Rand, particularly in her widely read novel from 1943, *The Fountainhead*. The story centres on the figure of Howard Roark, an architect who scorns the historical models and established rules. Instead he creates designs that are wholly personal and original: his guiding principle is authenticity, being true to himself. Roark was supposedly modelled on the architect Frank Lloyd Wright, but such authenticity was equally a core value of nineteenth-century musical aesthetics, associated in particular with Beethoven. Perhaps that is why we are told that Roark had always wanted to write music, and at one point he speaks of architecture as 'music in stone'.

The novel revolves round the contrast between Roark and his academically successful but ultimately uncreative architectural rival, Peter Keating, who eventually asks Roark to help him out with his own, crowning architectural project. Roark agrees, but on condition that no changes are made to his design. Keating, however, tones it down, and Roark responds by dynamiting the building. This leads to a trial at which Roark's impassioned defence of architectural authenticity leads the jury to acquit him. (He also gets the girl, Dominique Francon, who has married Keating but now leaves him in disgust.) As journalist Jonathan Freedland writes, 'Rand lionises the alpha male capitalist entrepreneur, the man of action who towers over the little people and the pettifogging bureaucrats – and gets things done

... Hers is an ideology that denounces altruism, elevates individualism into a faith and gives a spurious moral licence to raw selfishness.'[7] And seventy years later, American admirers of Rand's work range from Silicon Valley CEOs to Republican politicians. It's not just because of the way she lionises the alpha male. Rand also advocated rolling back the state and eliminating social support for the poor and vulnerable in order to prioritise exceptional individuals; though she had drawn on an artistic practice to make her point, her influence fed into the mythologisation of the entrepreneur as the hero of modern society. Nowadays Carlyle's Great Man theory is firmly ensconced in the world of boardrooms and soaring CEO remuneration.

On the eastern side of the Atlantic, Rand's fans include former Chancellor of the Exchequer Sajid Javid and Brexiteer Daniel Hannan (aka Baron Hannan of Kingsclere). Moreover her values resonate in *Britannia Unchained* (2012), a short book authored by a number of right-wing MPs who achieved prominence after Brexit – including Liz Truss, Johnson's blink-and-you'll-miss-it successor, whose strategy of transferring wealth from the poor to the rich in the name of economic growth was straight out of the Rand script.[8] (The Labour MP Jon Cruddas described *Britannia Unchained* as espousing 'a destructive economic liberalism that threatens the foundations of modern conservatism', adding that 'the bottom line for these Tory radicals is that the notion of community, society or indeed country is always trumped by textbook economic liberalism'.[9]) There are also resonances with *The Sovereign Individual*, a book first published in 1997 by American financial advisor James Dale Davidson and (Lord) William Rees-Mogg, one-time editor of the *Telegraph* and father of Jacob, the radical Brexiteer sometimes described by parliamentarians as the Honourable Member for the Eighteenth Century. It describes a twenty-first century in which digital technology and cryptocurrencies result in the disappearance of nation states. Freed from 'the oppression of government', genius is unleashed: a cosmopolitan 'cognitive elite' of 'truly Sovereign Individuals' will be able to 'realise full individual autonomy and independence'.[10] In this brave new world there will be extreme disparities of wealth, and social welfare will no longer exist.

This curious blend of economic analysis and science fiction represents asocial individualism with a vengeance, and resonates in turn with what in the 1960s Canadian sociologist C. B. Macpherson dubbed 'possessive individualism'. According to this account, the individual 'is free inasmuch as he is proprietor of his person and capacities. The human essence is freedom from dependence on the wills of others, and freedom is a function of possession.'[11] In effect this amounts to freedom without obligation, and again Boris Johnson provides a pertinent example: when he was eighteen, his housemaster at Eton noted with remarkable prescience that 'he honestly believes that it is churlish of us not to regard him as an exception, one who should be free of the network of obligation which binds everyone else'.[12] And historian David Runciman writes that 'as British society has become more unequal it has created pockets of privilege whose inhabitants are tempted to think that the normal rules don't apply to them'.[13] Like Roark – like Beethoven – they transcend the rules that govern the little people. I will return to freedom without obligation when I come to discuss Covid-19.

In the 1980s all these influences converged in the rise of the neoliberal ideology that advocates not only the rolling back of the state, the cutting of social support, and the fetishisation of the entrepreneur, but also a new definition of freedom. In political theorist Wendy Brown's words, 'neoliberal rationality reduces the meaning of freedom and autonomy to unimpeded market behavior'.[14] This is the textbook economic liberalism to which

Cruddas referred: the market knows best. And the technocratic, business-friendly system of global capitalism has resulted in a world of spiralling inequity between super-rich and super-poor – inequity that only increases with every successive disaster, whether or not generated by the global financial system.

Neoliberalism was instituted as the taken-for-granted economic ideology by economists, such as Milton Friedman, whose business was to model cycles of national or international wealth and poverty in terms of the interaction of market forces. Such models are based on a restricted number of selected indicators; people count only as statistics that feed algorithms. In that sense market forces are conceived as impersonal, disconnected from the agency of individuals. And here we get back to music. What in traditional music studies is called style history is conceived as the same kind of impersonal force. Compositional style is seen as advancing through cumulative technical development and the occasional paradigm shift. Composers are seen as discovering new possibilities in sound much as EV battery engineers discover new possibilities in previously untried materials – discover, not invent, because the possibilities were always latent in the materials. In fact the Great Men of music history have sometimes been thought of as acting at the behest of these impersonal forces. Schenker (who in this case had been reading Kant) wrote of the spirit of 'Nature' or 'Music' speaking through Beethoven, guiding his pen as he introduced the Lydian mode into his string quartet Op. 132 – even though he had no conscious intention of borrowing from the ancient modal system.[15] Seen this way, what marked out Beethoven as a genius was his access to a higher, superhuman realm.

Ultimately, then, music (or Music) unfolds from its inner resources, and as such its progression is preordained. From the beginning the idea of style history was entangled with evolutionary thinking, while the idea of music unfolding from within, generating the forward march of progress, is in line with the kind of history that derived from Georg Wilhelm Friedrich Hegel and was highly influential during the nineteenth century and into the twentieth. (Oswald Spengler's notorious model of history as recurrent cycles of national emergence and decline is a variation on the same theme.) This may sound like something from another age, if not another planet, but Russia's invasion of Ukraine – launched just after I started this book – shows otherwise.

In a speech given in February 2021, a year before his armies invaded Ukraine, Vladimir Putin said that 'in nature as in society, there is development, climax and decline. Russia has not yet attained its highest point. We are on the way.'[16] He was referencing previous Russian thinkers such as Ivan Ilyin and Lev Gumilev, who advanced the idea of a linguistically and culturally based Russianness that represents the antithesis of Enlightenment rationalism – a force, they claimed, that is destined to triumph over the West. Putin aims to make Russia great again by recreating the authentic nation of Tsar Peter the Great; that is the perspective from which he insists that Ukraine is an integral part of a greater Russia, and as such is not – can never be – a sovereign country. The idea of destiny lies at the heart of such thinking, and was behind the deluded beliefs that the Ukrainians would greet the Russian armies as liberators and Kyiv would fall within days. At the same time, in bringing destiny to fruition, Putin – no less than Schenker's Beethoven – marks himself out as the agent through whom history unfolds. Not understanding this way of thinking goes far to explain why the Western powers so long mistook Putin for a pragmatist they could do business with.

In this way world history comes to be seen as a kind of epic drama played out by historical forces that unfold their own destiny, working through those alpha males, the Great Men. Everybody else

– the mass of little people – is denied agency; for Putin, as for all conspiracy theorists, 'people are all puppets, moved around great chess boards'.[17] (Hence his astonishing lack of concern for civilian lives.) It is the same worldview as the nineteenth-century Western musical historiography in which change is generated by the unfolding of stylistic forces that work through the geniuses – in Rand's terms, the musical entrepreneurs. In music history, to be sure, the effects are not quite as deadly, though still bad enough (a disregard of audiences; a view of performers as mere technicians that undermines their self-respect, job satisfaction, and even mental health; and a wildly skewed conception of what music is and might be). But it is striking that the values and mentalities that today imperil the world and its peoples were already at work in the musical world of 200 years ago.

Music, Nostalgia, Delusion

People sometimes say a smell can take you straight back to places and events from childhood, and music has something of the same power. Castaways on *Desert Island Discs* often choose songs that remind them of a particular, emotionally charged occasion; a statistical analysis of their choices shows that they disproportionately choose music they encountered between the ages of ten and thirty, that is, during the years when they were forming their self-identity.[1] Composers write music to evoke the sounds and atmosphere of places from their past life: in 1885–6 Frederick Delius spent a year managing his father's orange plantation on the banks of the Mississippi, and over the ensuing fifteen years wrote a series of compositions that evoked aspects of its sound world. As a later newspaper interview had it, 'Delius used to sit at nightfall on the verandah, smoking and listening to the beautiful, harmonic singing of the negroes.'[2] As so often, the Black man's servitude is the white man's idyll.

All this is to say that music can be a powerful vehicle of personal nostalgia. It can also evoke more distant pasts. Maurice Ravel's *La Valse*, written in 1920 as a ballet score but more familiar as a concert piece, is set in 1850s Vienna; Carl Orff's *Carmina Burana*, so named after the medieval poetry collection from which its texts are taken, draws on pseudo-medieval chant, late Renaissance melodies, and a dash of Stravinsky to create an idealised image of the middle ages. And such musical time-travelling acquires social and political significance when it is used to evoke a past that in some way legitimises the present, for example through strengthening a sense of national identity. Japan's ancient and iconic court music, *gagaku*, has been repeatedly reinvented, most recently under the late nineteenth-century Meiji regime that also brought Westernisation to Japan: another part of the Meiji *gakunin*'s job was to play polkas. But the invention of tradition is most readily seen in the visual arts. Jacques-Louis David's *Brutus Receiving the Bodies of his Sons* – painted shortly after the outbreak of the French Revolution – is based on an episode from ancient Roman history, but is (and was) easily read

Figure 5. Jacques-Louis David, *Brutus Receiving the Bodies of His Sons* (1789). The story is that the sons of Lucius Junius Brutus, who founded the Roman Republic, conspired to overthrow it and reinstate the monarchy. Loyalty to the Republic compelled Brutus to order his sons' execution. Louvre Museum, Paris

as supporting French republicanism (Figure 5). In effect it placed the French republican movement at the centre of European history, representing it as the upholding of democracy and freedom – values seen as having originated in the classical world, the cradle of Western civilisation. It was in that sense creating an instant history that legitimised the present.

In this section I bring together music and the greatest convulsion in recent British politics (one that resonates with much that has happened elsewhere, particularly in America); my aim is to identify some underlying features that link them. Brexit, the UK's departure from the EU, was supported by a small majority of voters in the 2016 referendum, and implemented in 2020, though acrimonious disputes over the terms of the UK's departure still drag on as I write. One of its sources was a nostalgia for Englishness (and I mean Englishness, not Britishness) – a supposedly unchanging national essence enshrined particularly in the immemorial tradition of folksong. The idea goes back to the turn of the twentieth century. Metropolitan and upper-class collectors, many of them members of the English Folksong Society and several of them women, went into the countryside – or summoned rural singers to their country houses – and transcribed what they heard into staff notation. They eliminated verbal crudities and added piano accompaniments: the songs were gentrified, turned into 'art'-musical evocations of a pastoral never-neverland – an idealised, timeless, nostalgically valued England that had never really existed in the first place. That is why Dave Harker called his book on the collectors *Fakesong*.[3]

The principal ideologue of the Society was Cecil Sharp, in whose writings there are resonances not only of nationalism but also of racial science:

> If every English child be placed in possession of all these race-products, he will know and understand his country and his countrymen far better than he does at present; and knowing and understanding them he will love them the more, realise that he is united to them by the subtle bond of blood and kinship, and become, in the highest sense of the word, a better citizen, and a truer patriot.[4]

Also active in the English Folksong Society was the composer Ralph Vaughan Williams (Figure 6), who incorporated the folk songs he collected into compositions such as his *English Folksong Suite* of 1923–4. In this way he perpetuated and added cultural weight to what had come to be seen as an identity-defining national tradition.

But it's not just the timeless past. When I was at school in 1960s England, history lessons almost always seemed to revolve around the Tudors, under whom – as I learned – England was consolidated as an independent power whose influence increasingly extended far beyond its geographical limits. The story of the British empire might be traced back to such figures as the explorer, privateer, and slave

Figure 6. Ralph Vaughan Williams (right) and Gustav Holst in the Malvern hills, September 1921. Photograph by William Gillies Whittaker

trader (Sir) Francis Drake, who circumnavigated the globe in 1577–80; nearly a century later, in 1659, his exploits off the north-eastern coast of South America were celebrated in a masque, with music by Matthew Locke, that represented him as a pioneer of English expansionism. And Vaughan Williams's musical construction of Englishness drew not just on folksong but also on the elite music of the Tudor period (for example his *Fantasia on a Theme by Thomas Tallis* from 1910). History also merged with nature, as in another iconic emblem of Englishness: Vaughan Williams's rural 'romance' *The Lark Ascending*, which topped the poll when listeners to *Desert Island Discs* voted for the record they would take with them to the desert island.[5] Through his music, and that of other composers of the so-called 'cowpat' school, the disappearing England of a largely imaginary past was recreated, in the patriotic imagination drowning out the real but unappealing soundscape of twentieth-century British modernity. It was also part of Vaughan Williams's programme, and that of his contemporaries, to re-establish a distinctively English tradition of composition after a century during which continentals had dubbed Britain the 'land without music'. (Actually Britain had a rich musical culture at the time, but that was because it could afford to import the best continental musicians.)

The Tudor period didn't just inform Vaughan Williams's musically constructed version of Englishness. It is there in the Brexiteer lexicon of pluck, buccaneering, and punching above one's weight. Perhaps the most highly mythologised event in the whole of English history is Drake – again

"THERE IS TIME TO FINISH THE GAME AND BEAT THE SPANIARDS TOO."
SAID DRAKE

Figure 7. Drake at Plymouth Hoe (from H. E. Marshall, *Our Island Story*, 1905)

Drake – playing a game of bowls as the Spanish Armada is sighted off Plymouth Hoe, at which point he remarks that there is time to finish the game and beat the Spaniards too. Figure 7 is one of any number of representations of the scene. It has everything. There is Drake's cool, a sixteenth-century anticipation of James Bond (himself, according to historian Mike Finn, 'the living embodiment of Britain's self-delusion').[6] There is the contrast between the invincible Armada and Drake's woefully outnumbered navy, the epitome of pluck and punching above one's weight (though in reality it was the unseasonable August storms that did the heavy lifting). As for buccaneering, the Spanish considered Drake a pirate and put a price of 20,000 ducats – today about £6 million – on his head. The Brexit narrative places the EU in a tradition of foreign invaders, and the Brexiteers in a tradition of British heroes from Drake to Wellington to Churchill. This is the background to the absurd and offensive parallel Boris Johnson drew between Brexit and the war in Ukraine, so casting the EU in the role of Putin's Russia.[7]

It's not just music and pictures that feed patriotic nostalgia. Figure 7 comes from *Our Island Story*, a historical story book for children written – perhaps tellingly in Australia – by the British author Henrietta Marshall, and published in London in 1905, at the height of the Edwardian period (American editions were called *An Island Story*).[8] Exactly a century later, in 2005, the right-wing think tank Civitas republished it, with the stated aim of ensuring there was a copy in every school throughout the land. Conservative politicians endorsed it. In 2010 then Prime Minister David Cameron (who unleashed the Brexit referendum in order to quell tensions within the Conservative Party) named *Our Island Story* as his favourite childhood book. In the same year

Michael Gove, one of the original Brexiteers, borrowed its title for his speech 'All pupils will learn our island story', in which he prescribed a renewed emphasis on national history in schools.[9] And two years later, when the *Daily Express* launched its pro-Brexit 'crusade' (now casting the EU as infidels), it described Britain as 'a realm with a glorious island story stretching back a thousand years'. The same idea of national destiny that motivates Putin's war in Ukraine became palpable when Daniel Hannan, that admirer of Ayn Rand, wrote that after Brexit 'the past 40 years, during which we tore up our traditional trading relationships and artificially redirected our trade to Europe, will be seen as an aberration'.[10]

One reason that music matters is that it imprints patterns of thought and feeling from an early age. I remember from my childhood a long piece of paper that you placed behind the keys of your piano; if I remember rightly, at the top it read 'This is the house of Mrs Middle C', with a long curly bracket beneath it encompassing the entire keyboard, then below that smaller brackets picking out the C major scale within each octave, and below *that* still smaller brackets picking out C major triads; whether or not it has anything specifically to do with racism, learning classical music certainly reinforces a hierarchical mindset. Again, you might think of music as a sonified form of dance through which physical behaviours that distinguish different cultures are instilled – such as different kinds of gait and different ways of holding or moving the body, which in turn link with different mentalities and emotionalities (if there is such a word). Music helps to ground culture in the body. People speak about the Edwardian swagger of Elgar's music, an idea that encompasses not only sonorous and physical qualities but also the brazen self-confidence that marked British culture in the so-called glory days of the Empire before the 1914–18 war (a quality, ironically, that Elgar himself lacked). Such patterns of feeling – maybe it would be better to say such patterns of being – endure into later life.

And one of the reasons children's histories matter is that they do something similar. In 1994 the novelist Penelope Lively (born 1933) published *Oleander, Jacaranda*, an account of her childhood in Egypt. In it she recalls that *Our Island Story*

> had glossy romantic pictures of national heroes, with potted accounts of the finer moments of the nation's rise to pink glory. Boadicea and King Arthur and Sir Walter Raleigh and Kitchener and Queen Victoria all somehow rolled into one to produce essence of Englishness ... I look back in dismay. There has

been a lot of unlearning to do. And can it all be unlearned?[11]

In the case of the Brexiteers, at least, it seems not. For them, Marshall conjures up an England whose national destiny is to be less European than global. In her view the key event of English history – the bedrock of English difference – was the break with Rome, the very archetype of taking back control (Dominic Cummings's masterful Brexit slogan, also the name of a 2006 single by the American rock band Sparta). Marshall stoked the sense of exceptionalism that had its origin in imperial ideology, and was built into the tradition of Western 'art' music and the way it is thought about. All this fed into Brexit.

Nostalgia is more an emotional than a cognitive construct, which means it can act as a target of affective investment, self-identity, loyalty, or love (or hate), even as its rational content is underdefined or non-existent. That applies to music too. Consider what people mean when they talk about the 'musical' quality of political rhetoric. In his wartime speeches Churchill used inflections of rhythm, dynamics, tone and emphasis together with compositional devices such as repetition and climax-building to shape a message that was as compelling for how he said it as for what he said. He created meaning in the very act of performance. Martin Luther King did the same. Another iconic example is the voice of Saruman as depicted in J. R. R. Tolkien's *The Lord of the Rings*: it enchants his listeners, for whom all that it says seems wise and reasonable, awakening in them the desire 'by swift agreement to seem wise themselves'.[12] And here we encounter another of music's characteristic effects. Traditional critics often maintained that you could not change a single note of great music without ruining it: everything had to be just as it is. The musicality of Saruman's voice brings with it the same hypnotic quality of apparent inevitability. Music transforms a simple statement (e.g. 'X did not happen') into the unfolding of some deeper force ('X was not to be'). It is the voice of destiny, the foundation of music's power to naturalise, to rule out alternatives, to make it seem that the status quo cannot be other than it is.

Of course, the principle of effective oratory is supposed to be that you use the musical dimensions of speech to parse, selectively underline, animate, and project a message that is not only emotive but also cognitively coherent, based on considered analysis of real-world issues. The problem with today's post-truth politics is not that it is performative but that it is nothing but performative. Tolkien tells us that those who heard Saruman 'could seldom report the words that they heard; and if they did, they wondered, for little power remained in them'. As political sociologist William Davies puts it, in post-truth politics words have 'broken completely free of their factual moorings'.[13] They have, in short, turned into a kind of music, a sonic vehicle of persuasion that leaves no cognitive residue, and in which distinctions between truth and untruth have no purchase. Truth becomes what you can make people believe, or at least get away with.

In 2002 an unnamed senior political strategist in George W. Bush's White House (thought to be Karl Rove) mocked those who think that solutions to political problems emerge from the 'judicious study of discernible reality', and continued, 'that's not really the way the world works anymore ... We're an empire now, and when we act, we create our own reality ... We're history's actors.'[14] It's the word 'actors' that gives the game away. Post-truth politics is as much an arena for role-playing as the theatrical or operatic stage, or those online games where you are whoever you say you are. Johnson seizes upon the Ukraine war to role-play Churchill. Or, as a celebrity politician, he role-plays himself: Boris stars as 'Boris'. (His family call him 'Al', short for his real first name, Alexander; Boris – one of his several middle names, which he started using when he went 'up' to Oxford – is in effect a stage name.) Meanwhile Liz Truss role-plays Margaret Thatcher: that is how she sold herself to the 80,000 or so Conservative Party members who made her Prime Minister following Johnson's resignation. In such spectacular politics, Davies writes, 'everything is in the delivery, and the lasting contribution is neither here nor there'.[15]

In this way music is a model for the normalisation of fantasy worlds disconnected from and unconstrained by reality – worlds that range from Putin's Kremlin to Trump's White House, and from QAnon to those American states in which a majority still believe the Democrats stole the 2020 election. Such worlds are echo chambers, created through feedback loops of mutual persuasion, as was the fantasy that drove the UK out of the EU: science-fiction writer William Gibson described cyberspace as 'a consensual hallucination', and so was Brexit.[16] It's like those children's stories where you draw a cat and it springs off the page, or the way Humpty Dumpty uses words to mean whatever he says they mean: in one of those Latin tags that Johnson affects, it's not *cogito ergo sum* but *cogito ergo est* (I think, and therefore it is so). Or it's like the partying that went on at 10 Downing Street while the rest of the UK was in lockdown, as shown by Johnson's defence: it hadn't occurred to him, he said, that events where groups of people were drinking, conducting quizzes, or wearing tinsel might be considered to be parties.

The problem is that what is fantasy in music is delusion in politics. It's the difference between the timelessly rural England evoked by Vaughan Williams and those sunlit uplands to which Brexit was supposed to lead. It also explains what journalist Rafael Behr meant when, playing on the election slogan that helped sweep Johnson to power, Behr described him as 'getting [Brexit] done in the realm of pure imagination'.[17]

Music and
Administered Society

In 2007 I was involved in uncovering the Hattogate scandal, in which numerous recordings by leading pianists were fraudulently reissued under the name of Joyce Hatto. This led me to explore some classical music usenet groups, where suspicion of Hatto first emerged, and I was astonished at the extent of the flaming and trolling that was going on in them. Contrary to its public image, parts of the classical music world are pervaded by extreme intolerance, as Daniel Leech-Wilkinson has documented in his study of *Gramophone* record reviews.[1] This arises in part out of the widespread prejudices that Leech-Wilkinson identifies – against people of colour, women, LGBTQ communities – but also out of a combination of deep, identity-defining views and the lack of an adequate language for their expression. The culture of Western 'art' music does of course

86

have its own professional metalanguage, the purpose of which is precisely to enable the constructive exchange and negotiation of views between trained musicians. But that metalanguage is primarily based on notation, and the issue of how and in what sense notes on paper represent music is a fraught one.

Western classical music, at least as it has existed since around 1800, is constituted more as a world of things than of actions. Musical works can be seen as compositional labour condensed into a fixed textual form. Notation has a long history in the West, effectively beginning in the eleventh century. At that time it served as a memory aid to ensure correct performance. But gradually – and here I am telescoping centuries into a few sentences – notation became a means of imagining new music into existence, as well as of performing music you hadn't previously encountered. In jazz there are minimalist scores called lead sheets that enable musicians to play music they don't actually know (that is why collections of them are called 'fake books'); they aren't intended to be reproduced note by note, but rather used as a basis for idiomatic performance in jazz style. During the two centuries before 1800 much music circulated in a comparable form known as figured bass, a shorthand basis for partly extemporised performance.

But there was a continuing urge to notate music more exhaustively, reflecting the developing conception of the musical work as something that could be fully worked out on paper – something that had a permanently fixed form, just as a painting does. (Philosopher Lydia Goehr entitled her influential book on this development *The Imaginary Museum of Musical Works*.[2]) The change that took place around 1800 was essentially ontological – it revolved around what sort of thing music was considered to be – and it coincided with a change in how music was used. Before then, little music was expected to have a shelf life of more than a few years; part of the ontological change was the idea of a steadily growing canon of immortal masterpieces. The sexism of that term is not accidental. We have come back to the ideology of musical autonomy with which I began, the regime under which women are not creators but reproducers.

This way of thinking about music – as the production of permanently valuable objects rather than an intrinsically valuable real-time practice – was never an accurate representation of what actually happens in the culture of classical (or perhaps any other) music. It gave rise to the historiography built around musical works and marginalising audiences, performers, amateurs, and women – the people whose activities constitute music as a practice rather than as a stockpiling of products. (You would never guess from those old-fashioned histories of classical music that over the past 200 years the performance of pre-existing compositions has occupied a much larger role in the actual practice of music than the creation of new ones.) All this exaggerated the perceived difference between Western classical music and practically any other musical culture, Western or otherwise. But in recent decades there has been a pushback against this entire way of thinking. Alongside or instead of talking about music – the noun – musicologists increasingly talk about musicking – a verb, coined in 1987 by composer and educator Christopher Small, that encompasses all dimensions of music-making. This resonates with a broader shift in the human sciences from talking about objects to talking about practices; anthropologist Tim Ingold even talks about humaning ('to human', he says, 'is a verb').[3] And just as talk about musicking might be seen as a reaction against the depersonalised idea of style history, so I don't think it's fanciful to see talk about humaning as a reaction against the reification of social relationships epitomised by neoliberalism.

Paradoxically, the ideology of music's autonomy and transcendence coincided with its commodification. Seen as an enduring entity defined by writing – a musical text – music entered the marketplace. It could be bought, sold, or rented out; a key factor in the development of the post-1800 regime of the musical work was the mass take-up of the piano as a domestic instrument for amateurs, creating a huge market for printed music to play on it. Music could be protected by copyright, and today the catalogues of major artists such as Tina Turner are investment opportunities. The score becomes a kind of contract to which performers can be held, much as a builder can be held to the architect's drawings (which themselves form part of the contract). But just as the deeply collaborative nature of music is misrepresented by seeing it as exclusively the work of composers, so thinking of music as writing distorts it: if the text is what can be legally protected, then everything that isn't in the text is implicitly devalued. (Even recordings, which aren't as drastically reductive as scores, misrepresent as fixed something that is created anew every time it is performed.) The problem with this lies not so much in scores as such, but in the way they are thought of as embracing everything – or everything that matters – in music. Seeing them that way misrepresents what both music and scores are.

The relationship between music that is written down and oral (or aural) music – music that is transmitted and performed without notation – has long been at the centre of the nearest thing to a culture war in music. The jazz and rock keyboardist Ben Sidran spoke of 'literate' versus 'oral man' (and woman, but Sidran originally wrote this in 1981), and of the 'peculiarly "black" approach to rhythm'.[4] And a page earlier he had written that 'utter misunderstanding has been at the heart of the relationship between black and white America'. Binary divisions stack up: oral vs literate, black vs white, jazz vs classical, improvised vs composed, collective vs authored. It's like *fin-de-siècle* Vienna, where musically interpretable qualities like structural vs decorative and creative vs imitative resonated with broader cultural binaries such as natural vs artificial, deep vs superficial, or masculine vs feminine – and, beneath all these, Gentile vs Jew. That was the logic of Viennese antisemitism. It is how culture wars work.

Jazz drummer Max Roach once said that in Western classical music 'there's two people who control everything – that's the composer and the conductor . . . The chorus, they're a bunch of serfs, the whole orchestra, that's serfs; these people are like slaves – they just do the bidding of this one person who has written it and this conductor who is the "driva man," so to speak.'[5] ('Driva man' refers to the white overseers of Black workers in plantations, and is the title of one of Roach's songs.) And in an article about urban planning, academic lawyer Dean Rowan writes that the traditional, rational approach to planning 'has musical analogs in strict allegiance to the composer's score and obeisance to the hierarchical command of the conductor'.[6] In contrast to this, he continues, are radical approaches that 'vibrantly accord with improvisational methods, employing practices of active listening, alleviation of oppressive hierarchy, and invitation and acceptance of differences'. The very vocabulary expresses the association of classical music with the status quo, bureaucracy, and social exclusion in contrast to that of jazz with progress, social justice, and inclusion. It is at bottom a contrast between repression and freedom.

Suggesting a link between notated music – in particular Western classical music – and repression is not so unreasonable. I already noted how classical music is tied up with hierarchical thinking. Schenker despised democracy. Robert Adlington and Esteban Buch associate classical music with 'a nostalgia for ... pre-democratic orders of government',[7] while Anna Bull shows how classical music reproduces and reinforces the values of white middle-class culture.[8] Geoffrey Baker speaks of the militaristic regimes that sustain orchestral performance, while Leech-Wilkinson (who spoke of music performing the right in culture) provides copious examples of how classical music students are indoctrinated with the idea that there are fixed, historically sanctioned ways in which the music must be played. That would be a perfect example of conservative nostalgia – maintaining the past unchanged – if it wasn't for the fact that today's obligatory performance style is nothing like how music was performed before the mid twentieth century. Today's classical music is almost an invented tradition.

As Leech-Wilkinson shows, performance is policed by conservatory examinations and the structures through which performers are hired, as well as by the intolerance of critics. And both he and Bull note the link, characteristic of authoritarian regimes, to the flood of sexual abuse charges that have emanated from specialist music schools. There are also those on the far right who invoke Western classical music in support of white supremacism: on the Neo-Nazi internet forum Stormfront, a contributor under the carefully chosen name 'Karajan' (the famous conductor was at one time a member of the Nazi party) challenges readers to 'listen to more classical music . . . The more you listen to it, the more you understand that such beauty, such majesty, can only be the work of white[s] FOR WHITES . . . Only if we fail to insure the survival of our white race will the beauty of classical music disappear.'[9]

But both Roach and Rowan go off the rails when they simply identify repression with written and freedom with unwritten music. For them, it seems, a musical score is a product specification to be executed to exacting standards under the supervision of the conductor, who carries primary responsibility for quality control. But the way musicians use scores is not in the least like that. Even in the case of canonic repertory, the score is a minimalist representation of the music you hear. It may not be quite as minimal as a jazz lead sheet, but it is still heavily reliant on what its users are assumed to know before they ever pick it up. It strips out emotion, the body, real-time action and interaction. Between paper and sound come complex and crucial processes of musicianly interpretation that require not just manual dexterity but deep stylistic knowledge, the ability to listen to others, and – in the case of an orchestra – empathetic response to the conductor's own interpretive vision. In short, the score strips out what audiences actually hear: the performance.

Conversely (as Roach, at least, was well aware), jazz is not simply put together on the spur of the moment. Or rather it is – but put together out of the multitude of tropes and patterns that jazz musicians internalise in a lifetime of performing and listening (aspiring jazz players spend long hours on their own, listening to and imitating records). Nor is it correct to think that notations play no part in jazz. It's not just the fake books. Louis Armstrong carefully wrote out some solos in 1923–4 for copyright purposes, and then 'improvised' them over the following years.[10] The supposedly watertight distinction of oral vs literate – or improvisation vs composition, or creative vs imitative – is just as socially constructed and just as leaky as that between Black and white.

Nor is it just Sidran and Rowan. Many post-1945 composers and theorists – the two went together, with 'composer/theorist' being a common job title in American universities – were of a rationalist bent, and thought of music in terms of patterns or structures of notes, sometimes conceived visually or mathematically. (This is the reverse engineering I referred to earlier.) They thought of music being made up of notes in the way that material objects are made up of atoms, or half-tone images are made up of dots.

But think of Jimi Hendrix improvising, or the singing of Kate Bush or Maria Callas, or the florid singing of South India: in each case, you might say that the sound passes *through* different pitch values (imagine a graph), but it's not like a string of beads, one note after another. The notes aren't *in* the singing, it's rather that you can think of it that way for purposes of representation or measurement. They are a construct of trained listening – what used to be called 'ear training' – in other words, listening oriented towards the identification of musical objects. The problem, as music theorist Christopher Hasty has said,[11] is when you think not just that the notes are really there in the music, but that they are *all* that is there. Hasty has criticised theorists of modernist music – his own specialism – for concentrating on patterns of notes at the expense of all the other things that happen in music; the point of analysing patterns of notes, he says, is to see how they interact with everything else – rhythms, dynamics, textures, timbres, and so forth. Otherwise you are constructing a reduced, rationalised model of the world, and then behaving as if that rationalised model really *was* the world.

That is one possible definition of the elusive phenomenon we call modernity. It is also a way to make the world too simple, create excessive certainty, and become dangerously over-confident. It is the same over-confidence that spills out of *Britannia Unchained* with its black-and-white model of the Conservative utopia (or dystopia) that Liz Truss struggled to put into practice for a few weeks until her government collapsed. And it is a context within which music can offer a perspective on today's rationalised, administered world. Sociologist Rob Shields speaks of how the rationalisation of business has led to dehumanisation, using the example of top-down management: the assumption, he says, is that 'all knowledge or understanding is held by the instruction-giver', whereas 'in reality, managers depend on having *knowledgeable* employees who possess their own capacity to synthesise information given in instructions with their own experience and networks of information'.[12] Another way to put this is that managers need to respect their employees, where respect is a two-way relationship.

The rationalised business model is how Rowan assumes that orchestras work, but in fact represents exactly how they *don't* work. The old-fashioned image of the all-powerful conductor conveyed by the media is misleading. Good conductors mobilise the extremely high-level skills of their musicians, as far as possible devolving decision-making into (literally) their hands: good ensemble depends more on musicians listening to one another than on a magisterial baton technique. Fine-grained performance decisions have to be made, so to speak, at the coal face. And conductors who do not respect orchestral musicians – who do not give them the space to play at their best – will not be respected in return. The difference is audible.

Part of what makes top-down management systems dehumanising is that instead of being called upon to exercise judgement based on your skill, experience, and sensibility – instead of being involved as a person – you are turned into an artefact of the system, in effect a lab rat. Call-handling systems are dehumanising because you can't interact with them when none of the available options correspond to what you want; it's like being trapped inside a computer game. Road rage results from being cooped up in a metal box, isolated from other road users with whom you can communicate only crudely, quite possibly misinterpreting their actions or intentions. And, apart from the metal box, much the same applies to Facebook and Twitter, where people flame first and think second (if at all). Even orchestral music-making, despite what I said about respect, can be dehumanising when performers feel little investment in the end product;[13] job satisfaction is consistently higher in chamber music, where textures are transparent and everyone is in aural contact with everyone else. Such music offers an exquisitely sensitive environment for social interaction, for interpersonal intimacy, for empathy. In a word, it fosters what I call musical togetherness.

Musical Togetherness

Among music's powers for social good, probably the most frequently spoken of is its ability to induce bonding: music, like dance, creates a dimension of shared experience at both an inter-cognitive and an inter-corporeal level. Individuals diminish or merge their individual identities within a group identity – a shared musical identity – that emerges at a super-ordinate level. In Paradise, Nevada, a Mrs Orrico (whose heritage is Chinese/Japanese but who was brought up to think of herself as simply American) attended a concert by BTS, the K-pop boy band who were invited to the White House in 2022. The divisions of Covid-era America seemed to melt away: 'seeing people of all ages, seeing male, female, Black people, Asian people, Mexican', she said, 'grandpas, grandmothers, little kids, and everybody . . . There was nothing like hearing 40,000 people all singing along to the songs.' And she added, 'for that brief time, nothing else existed'.[1] Such bonding was much valued by Reformation leaders. Jewish turned Calvinist theologian Immanuel Tremellius wrote that 'singing together unites men, just like providing a chain in the mind'.[2] The same happens when music is used to support synchronised action in military contexts, lowering the thresholds of individual identity and so creating solidarity. Cognitive archaeologist Stephen Mithen makes the parallel with military contexts when he speaks of the evolutionary value of music.[3] And music psychologist Ian Cross emphasises something I mentioned earlier: music is more effective than language at creating a sense of unity, because its lack of denotative content means it can afford community among people who might be separated by the denotative specificity of language.[4] (In such contexts music foregrounds what people have in common, while language foregrounds what they don't.) Cross describes music as a tool for the management of uncertainty in group contexts, and sees this as central to its adaptive value.

I already referred to the problem with musical bonding. It involves group identity construction, and identity means difference from others. In the sixteenth century – and later – Protestants constructed their identity in opposition to Catholics. In the Brexit wars, Remainers constructed their identity in opposition to Leavers (and vice versa). Nationalism entails a shared identity differentiated from others. According to novelist John Le Carré, 'for nationalism you need enemies':[5] think of the Ukrainians, united in their opposition to Russia and so enacting the reality of Ukrainian nationhood. (This is the logic that leads populist politicians to make enemies of a vaguely defined 'elite' that somehow manages to not include the super-rich and party donors.) The same opposition was played out musically in the 2022 Eurovision Song Contest, with Russia banned and Ukraine's folk-rap Kalush Orchestra the winner thanks to a massive popular vote. And music is valued by alt-right groups not only because it can recruit disaffected white teenagers to the cause by giving them (in Nancy Love's words) 'a target, a purpose for their anger and rage',[6] but also because – like football – it creates 'In' groups defined by their opposition to 'out' groups. Such bonding turns music into an agent of division as much as of solidarity.

But this inherently divisive form of bonding is not what I mean by musical togetherness. Infant–carer communication – the intimate dialogue of sound and touch that is crucial for early socialisation, the development of a capacity for forming relationships and communicative expression – is not a matter of losing identity, but of gaining it in relation to a significant other. Similarly when researchers find that music accelerates the process of bonding, or predisposes people to like one another, that does not have to mean they lose themselves within an impersonal, monolithic 'us': it may rather mean the forging of dyadic interpersonal relationships that develop into a criss-crossing mesh, holding a group together in a manner less like Tremellius's chains than like the relational networks found in neuronal circuits and mycorrhizal ecosystems.

A major focus of musical togetherness is what psychologists Stephen Malloch and Colwyn Trevarthen call communicative musicality[7] – an umbrella term for an extensive variety of real-time musical interactions (of which infant–carer communication is one). An important element of this is entrainment: just as two people walking together may without knowing it fall into step with one another, so jazz musicians synchronise with one another through a process of give-and-take in which the beat is negotiated between the players. It's not that they are conforming to an external, mechanical beat (like soldiers being drilled, or musicians playing to a click track): the beat is elastic, flexible, and socially produced.

Figure 8. Jaleel Shaw (alto saxophone) and Roy Haynes (drums). Fountain of Youth Quartet performing at Dizzy's Club Coca-Cola, Lincoln Center, New York, 2007. Photograph by ZUMA. Alamy

Members of the groove section in a jazz ensemble – such as piano, string bass and drums – listen to one another and entrain particularly closely, but at the same time are in dialogue with the saxophone soloist who may push them on or pull them back (Figure 8). And the sense of keeping in time with one another engenders a specifically musical kind of intimacy; jazzmen (and women) liken it to being married. Nor is it just jazz. In classical music good 'ensemble' embraces such attunement in pitch, timing, dynamic balance, articulation, and sound quality. You can also hear it in the perfect concurrence and blending of Robert Plant's and Alison Krauss's voices in 'Your Long Journey' (from their 2007 album *Raising Sand*); no wonder the song sparked a rumour that there was a romantic relationship between them.

Another aspect of communicative musicality involves the sense of wave-like rising and falling of intensity characteristic of many (though certainly not all) genres of music, which translates into musical parameters such as temporal and dynamic shaping. Writing of how people experience the present moment, psychiatrist Daniel Stern describes everyday life as made up of a series of shaped narrative episodes each lasting a few seconds (he illustrates this through the thought processes of someone having breakfast and discovering they have run out of butter). Stern explains what he means by likening it to a musical phrase, which is 'felt to occur during a moment that is not instantaneous, but also not parcelled out in time into sequential bits like the written notes. Rather, it is a continuous, analogic, flowing whole occurring during a now.'[8]

To put it another way, music is shaped like human consciousness. It captures intimate qualities of personhood. And Stern stresses how important unwritten, small-scale nuance is in both music and life: 'the scale is small', he writes, 'but that is where we live'.[9] Such nuance is found in solo music, of course – think of the expressive performance of almost anything by Chopin – but in ensemble performance you hear it being negotiated between the performers. Stern speaks of how in everyday life people share a shaped moment with one another – in conversation for example – and calls this a 'feeling voyage'. That is an excellent description of what happens in the playing of jazz or string quartets, or what happened when Plant and Krauss sang together.

All these processes take place in real time, with individuals listening to other individuals in constantly shifting, networked patterns. Jazz is a genre that has developed around improvisation, which as I said does not mean everything is improvised from scratch but that space is created for improvisation. But this is also true of classical music in which musicians are playing from sheet music: the unwritten nuance I have just been talking about is shaped only in the moment. There, too, timing, dynamics and the rest emerge through interaction, through acts of mutual listening, and that is why – in the same way as in jazz – classical music creates togetherness. In that sense, like jazz players but less overtly, classical musicians improvise (Figure 9). And it is

Figure 9. String quartet in Oradea, Romania, 2016. Photograph by Larisa Birta. Reproduced under Creative Commons CC0 1.0 license

because of this ongoing, real-time interaction that the metaphor of conversation plays so prominent a part in talking about music. People have compared string quartets to civilised conversation since the eighteenth century, and the discourses of jazz are equally full of it.

Music therapy is also a practice of close listening and mutual interaction. It is particularly effective with clients who have communication problems, establishing a safe space – DeNora's 'asylum' – within which music facilitates the forging of relationship. Sometimes clients initially open themselves to the music, and only through that to the therapist. Joint improvisation between client and therapist can encourage the expression of emotion or trauma that the client could not put into words, so fostering confidence and the construction, or rebuilding, of stable identity. As I said, music encourages empathy, the ability to see, hear, and know the other by putting yourself in their place, and conversely to know yourself through the other's eyes and ears. In therapy these relational acts come to the fore, but they are equally present in jazz and classical chamber music: as sociologist Alfred Schutz wrote in 1951, a musician 'has not only to interpret his own part' but also 'the other player's interpretation of his – the other's – part and, even more, the other's anticipations of his own'.[10] That is why I refused to draw a clear line between 'aesthetic' and 'applied' music. And in all these cases music is a dimension of social life, but with the proviso that Tim Ingold and Elizabeth Hallam add after they use this term: they 'do *not* mean the life of some hypostatized, superorganic entity', they say, 'namely "society"'. Rather they mean 'those mutually constitutive relationships through which, as they grow older together', people 'continually participate in each other's coming-into-being'.[11] Relationships produce society, not the other way round.

Creativity theorist and jazz pianist Keith Sawyer has developed a schematic model of collaborative performance that he illustrates in terms of jazz improvisation. Suppose we have a group of jazz musicians. One of them – A – plays something. Given the more or less accepted norms of jazz style, this delimits a field of possible continuations, ruling out others. B responds, picking up on some aspects of what A played, and so opening up further possible ways of continuing while ruling out still others. And so they continue.[12] All the players share what Sawyer calls 'the referent' – a memory of what has been played and, based on that, a sense of what could happen next. The referent does not pre-date the act of performance; it is collaboratively produced in real time, and jointly owned. That is of course a very minimal description of jazz, but that is its strength. You could think of string quartet performance in the same terms. You would be working with a different set of norms, and the improvisatory element would mainly subsist in the transformation of the notes on the page into rhythmically, dynamically, and tonally shaped sounds. But the key points – the social production and collaborative ownership – remain. Whether it is jazz or classical music, then, you might think of what the players are doing in terms of the mutually constitutive relationships through which, as they grow older together, they continually participate in one another's coming-into-being.

Music, Covid, Ethics

It is too painful to list all the things that vitiated the handling of Covid-19, whether in the UK or elsewhere. But what I see as the most fundamental factor is the value system represented by neoliberalism, specifically the possessive individualism that I described as an ideology of freedom without obligation. Charles Taylor calls this the malaise of modernity, in his book of the same name.[1]

It is most overt in America. As expounded by Ayn Rand, developed by economists like Milton Friedman, and internalised by many Republican and Conservative politicians, it is a way of thinking that fetishises freedom understood in purely individualistic terms as a fundamental right that trumps all others (even though it is in reality freedom for a minority: in overturning *Roe v. Wade* the US Supreme Court signalled that a woman is less a free agent than a uterus on legs, while Tyler Stovall has shown how in America freedom has always meant white freedom).[2] The institutional correlate of the neoliberal individual is the publicly owned company, which imposes on its management the fundamental obligation to serve the interests of shareholders, effectively overriding those of customers, the larger public, and the environment. Neoliberalism takes to an extreme the eighteenth-century capitalist principle that self-interest drives economic development, and has resulted in gross and relentlessly growing inequities of wealth. Increasingly the rich are rentiers, profiting from assets rather than creating employment that pays reasonable wages and provides a measure of job security. Neoliberalism and technology are together responsible for the gig economy, which, as its name suggests, is an updated version of exploitative employment practices long widespread in the music industry.

Covid mercilessly exposed the lethal shortcomings of an ethical system that has the autonomous individual and possessive individualism at its core. Time and again it illustrated the principle of what I call 'Covid ethics': no one is safe until everyone is safe. I wear a mask to protect you, and in turn rely on you to wear a mask to protect me. It follows from this that *your* freedom to live as you like is incompatible with *my* freedom – quite simply – to live. Much the same applies to vaccination. The drastic skewing of risk according to age imposed on the young an obligation to curtail their freedom in order to protect the old, especially before the development of vaccines – after which there was a reciprocal obligation on the newly protected old to curtail their freedom in order to protect the as yet unvaccinated young. We have mutually intertwined obligations to one another. That is why, as SAGE committee member Stephen Reicher said, Covid is 'a "we" thing', not a 'me' thing.[3] And the phrase 'no one is safe until everyone is safe' was coined in relation to the extension of vaccination beyond the first world, a programme that is still far from meeting its targets: that too is a 'we' thing, not a 'me' thing – not least because unprotected populations are incubators of viral variants.

That's why it's simply inadequate to say, as in the UK many Conservative politicians did during the pandemic, that individual behaviour should be a matter of personal judgement. According to former minister (Sir) Desmond Swayne, we all have the right 'to make our own assessment of the risks we are prepared to take'.[4] In effect he is claiming the right to decide what risks the old and the immunosuppressed shall have forced on them. In 2021 economic

commentator Aditya Chakrabortty spoke of 'an ideology that claims to be about freedom when really it
means selfishness', and that 'sees any curtailment of
its liberties, no matter how justified or temporary,
as Stalin sending in the tanks' (though in 2022 it's
Putin we think of).[5] Such views were argued even
more trenchantly in America, where both masks and
vaccines became politicised; no wonder a contributor to the 'What you're doing' section of the *New
York Times*'s daily coronavirus newsletter wrote 'to
my fellow immuno-compromised Americans, if you
don't already know, . . . you're on your own now'.
And another contributor condemned 'this American
idea of personal freedom without regard for the
protection of the most vulnerable'. For the vulnerable, the conservative mantra of 'living with Covid'
all too easily translated into dying from Covid.

To me it is simply common sense that there can
be circumstances in which individual freedom
becomes unsustainable except at the cost of whole-
sale avoidable mortality, meaning that – for the
duration of these circumstances – it is reasonable
to subordinate freedom of the individual to the
freedom of the community. So I find it hard to
understand how the former Supreme Court judge
and Reith Lecturer (Lord) Jonathan Sumption –
sometimes dubbed 'the cleverest man in Britain'

– could describe the restrictions imposed because of Covid-19 as 'the most significant interference with personal freedom in the history of our country'. He added that they had turned England into a 'police state . . . This is how freedom dies.'[6] The problem with this is not just a value system that places the burden of temporary restrictions and an abstract conception of absolute freedom above people's lives. It's that freedom and constraint are not the appropriate terms in which to think about it. If wearing masks is a matter of mutual obligation, then – in Reicher's words – 'we can reframe the mask issue as something we do for each other rather than something that is done to us. Mask wearing thereby stops being an issue of autonomy and becomes an assertion of agency.'[7] As Charles Taylor says of the sense of inwardness that defines the modern Western self, because that's how we are it's hard to imagine being any other way.[8] Yet the hyper-individualism that leads people to see everything in terms of personal freedom is not a given. It is a choice.

Of course the scope of these ethical principles goes far beyond the pandemic. My belief that Brexit was a profoundly wrong path for the UK to take isn't based just on the lies, the divisiveness, or the economic madness: it's also because Brexit meant opting out of international networks of mutual obligation in favour of an 'England First' ideology, to borrow the title of a breakaway faction of the British National Front. In March 2022 a reader wrote to the *Guardian* that

> In contrast to the dead end of empire, European integration promises a commonwealth of independent nations rooted in consent, democracy, shared values and mutual cooperation in return for a degree of pooled sovereignty. Britain, cheered on by such Putin admirers as Nigel Farage and Donald Trump, has chosen to reject this postimperial model (one that has brought peace, prosperity and stability to Europe) in favour of its own sepia-tinged, nostalgia-driven version of a distant global past.[9]

But it is in relation to the climate emergency – and climate justice, with its racial dimension – that the ethics of mutual obligation becomes most pressing. Global weather systems are highly interdependent, and so climate change too is a 'we' thing. The obligations ramify in both space and time. There are the obligations of the so-called developed countries that created global warming to the countries of the Global South that have to date borne the brunt of it. But there are also the obligations of present-day national governments and the global fossil fuel industry to the future of the planet and the survival of humanity. In September 2022 – a few days before I wrote this – the US House Committee on Oversight and Reform released documents demonstrating big oil's lack of commitment to the carbon reduction goals it loudly claims to promote; Shell employees, for example, were told not to 'give the impression that Shell is willing to reduce carbon dioxide emissions to levels that do not make business sense'.[10] (This was on the same day that reports emerged of over fifty British climate campaigners who had blockaded an oil terminal partly owned by Shell being sent to jail.[11]) No wonder UN Secretary-General António Guterres recently spoke of the 'grotesque greed' of the fossil fuel companies.[12] But it goes beyond greed, on however spectacular a scale. It is not only obligation to others but also any but the shortest-term conception of self-interest that has gone out the window. Do oil company executives and shareholders not have children? Is human culture worth so little? What is the point of wealth on an uninhabitable planet? This is individualism pushed way beyond the bounds of responsibility or even comprehensibility.

And what might all this possibly have to do with music? I hope the answer is obvious. In a word: everything, because music constitutes a – perhaps the – outstanding working example of communally grounded selfhood in our midst. Think back to what I said about jazz ensembles and string quartets making music together: as long as the music lasts, they create a constantly renewed yet stable community based on close listening, recognition of the other, and mutual trust. Relationships within this community are built from the bottom up, and are in constant motion as bilateral or multilateral alignments between individuals follow on one another in kaleidoscopic succession (any classical string quartet is full of examples of this). Patterns of mutual listening change with them, and so social – which is also to say musical – cohesion is maintained. Musical togetherness is at the same time flexible and resilient; it does not easily lend itself to division or fragmentation in the manner of in-groups defined by opposition to or hatred of out-groups – the basic mechanism of nationalism, populism, and the culture wars. To be sure, there is space in music for agency and freedom, but it is not Sumption's or the libertarians' absolute freedom, nor the asocial – or anti-social – freedom of possessive individualism. It is agency and freedom *in relation to other people*, in short a relative and relational freedom that creates space for others.

Speaking of the West-Eastern Divan Orchestra, Daniel Barenboim once called music a 'practical utopia'. That is a perfect description of music therapy, which on the one hand affords a protected, non-physical asylum – less a place than a way of being – but on the other hand is a highly effective, *practical* means of restoring mental health and wellbeing with lasting effect. And the point is that all collaborative music-making involves the same values of recognition and mutual care. Michael Tree, the Guarneri Quartet's viola player, writes that in performance 'just about anything can happen' (and the final pages of *Indivisible by Four* – a book written by the Guarneri's first violinist – illustrate what Tree is talking about).[13] There is an element of the unknown in the performance of even the most familiar music that mandates the same kind of mutual trust as exists between mountaineers roped together. William Davies – for whom loss of trust lies at the heart of the UK's current political crisis – remarks that 'a modern liberal society is a complex web of trust relations'.[14] Collaborative musicking too is a complex web of trust relations, made audible.

But what happens when the music stops? Talk about music's potential to change the world for the better rarely addresses the question of just *how* it might do so, and this gives utopianism a bad name. I've argued that musicking creates socialities with highly desirable, humane characteristics that range from recognition of the other and mutual care and trust to the resilience that results from its basis in acts of mutual listening: musical socialities are built from the bottom up, exactly the point that Ingold and Hallam made (as I summarised it, relationships produce society, not the other way round). British composer James Saunders speaks of music as a 'sonification of dynamic interaction between people'.[15] Music is a privileged arena within which to understand the dynamics of social relationship, because it discloses relationship so clearly as sound. It strips out the contingencies from social relationship, exposing such elemental issues as the balance between the interests of the collective and the individual. And as I write this book academic interest in the socialities of musicking seems to be surging, especially among early-career researchers.

Saunders continues: 'at a time where communities are being separated, divisions are emphasized, and autocratic government is prevalent, work that explores how people might work together and reflect on social interaction has the potential to encourage positive social change'. I agree, yet the claim might provoke scepticism. For one thing, Saunders is talking about contemporary experimental music, and not so many people listen to that. For another, ensembles whose music embodies such progressive ideals don't always put them into practice outside music: plenty of string and jazz quartets have been run on principles that are closer to dictatorship than to democracy – and that, too, gives utopianism a bad name. We need to get real. Sadly, music is not a magic bullet. Ethical values don't seep from sound to social behaviour through some mysterious osmosis. Just as you can't assimilate a book by sleeping with it under your pillow, so any amount of listening to music – or even playing it – is in itself unlikely to make you a better member of society, nor will it change the system.

Yet music can instigate change. Here is an example: a study carried out by Ehud Bodner and Avi Gilboa showed how listening to 'crisis songs' (a genre of songs broadcast in Israel at times of national crisis) induced members of two often antagonistic groups – religious and secular Jews – to think more positively of one another.[16] Just thinking about the songs for a few minutes had a positive effect. The effect didn't, however, occur when the crisis songs were replaced by love songs. Analysis of the subjects' responses indicated that the songs induced a sense of sorrow and grief shared across a national community of feeling. Music mobilised subjects' thoughts and feelings, memories and expectations, so allowing for powerful effects of life history, culture, and context. And in the end it is this capacity of music to prompt thought as well as feeling that can make a difference. It's like what anthropologist Claude Lévi-Strauss said about food: music is good for thinking with. But for it to make a lasting difference you have to do the thinking and then act on it. Music can't change the world. Only people can do that.

In this section – in this book – I have aimed to show how thinking about music and the broader world in tandem can throw light on possible modes of harmonious coexistence and social belonging, and equally on pernicious modes of thinking and acting that have been so thoroughly naturalised in everyday life as to be taken for granted: as Marianna Ritchey says (in the book Bryan Parkhurst was talking about), 'neoliberal theory has become naturalized in US culture as common sense'.[17] It's like the systemic inequity that perpetuates racism yet is invisible to its beneficiaries. And just as, in Uwagba's words, 'Black people cannot ourselves abolish whiteness – white people will need to relinquish it',[18] so it is the beneficiaries of neoliberalism who will need to relinquish it. Perhaps the most cheering thing I have read in researching this book is that, in the recent words of former private wealth lawyer Stephanie Brobbey, 'a growing number of wealth holders . . . recognise that wealth inequality is destabilising our economy and endangering the fabric of our society. They are advocating for higher taxes on wealth.'[19] Meanwhile the corresponding obligation of society at large is to do what, at least in Britain, it did over drink driving: agree that the very idea of freedom without obligation is beyond the pale, and call out those who embrace it.

Activist historian Rebecca Solnit writes that 'the right have succeeded in reestablishing an economy of extreme inequality, but not a society fully committed to that inequality'.[20] And using an apt metaphor from music, she speaks of a shift from 'the autonomous individual of hypercapitalism and social darwinism to a recognition of both the natural and social worlds as orchestras of interdependence, of survival as an essentially collaborative and cooperative business'. I think she is absolutely right, but to properly understand what she is saying you have to know how orchestras work.

Pandemic Intimacy

I said that neoliberalism is built on the principle that people act only in their self-interest; I don't believe the 'only', but neoliberalism has done much to make it true. And everyday experience of the Covid-19 pandemic has shown up the limitations as well as the dangers of autonomous individualism. The pain of restricting contact with other people through wearing masks, social distancing, and lockdown, and the epidemic of mental illness to which it gave rise, vividly illustrates how humans construct selfhood out of social connectedness, their relationships with other people. The *New York Times* coronavirus newsletter was a rich source for people's experiences: one contributor said that in lockdown 'I fear I will lose my identity and individuality and continue to shrink into anonymity.' Another observed how everybody looked emotionless in masks, not quite human. On the one hand Covid summoned up people's willingness – their desire – to help one another, to care for one another; on the other hand it limited their ability to do just that, and to express their feelings both for and to one another.

Face-to-face musicking suffered particularly cruelly during the pandemic. A report by the Incorporated Society of Musicians documented the decimation of music in British schools.[1] The picture was equally bad for professional musicians: they were already reeling from the effects of Brexit, which made getting the visas for European tours a nightmare, and because most are self-employed they missed out on the furlough schemes introduced by governments. Some gave up touring in Europe; others abandoned their careers. There were experiments with socially distanced ensembles playing to socially distanced audiences, which resulted in a noticeably different sound; that makes the obvious but easily overlooked point that – at least until the development of amplified sound – music has been commonly conceived, and acoustically designed, for indoor performance by musicians in close physical proximity. And more to the point, socially distanced music could never be financially viable. Live performance was even more difficult for choirs: singing was thought to be highly efficient at spreading the virus. Near to Seattle a rehearsal of the Skagit Valley Chorale was identified as a super-spreader event, with thirty-three singers infected and two dying. One of the first and best documented of such events, it played a major part in the recognition by scientists of the crucial role that aerosols – rather than just droplets and contaminated surfaces – played in the spreading of Covid-19.[2]

Zoom helped people cope with lockdown, even if it sometimes made life resemble the dystopian world of J. G. Ballard's short story from 1977, 'The Intensive Care Unit'.[3] It provided a medium for real-time audio and video contact, not only through straight conversation but also through other modes of real-time interaction. Again the *New York Times* newsletter provides examples: a father and son had regular Zoom meetings where they listened together to albums by Phish; a mother and daughter arranged to buy the same ingredients and cook the same dish once a week, chatting over Zoom while they cooked; a grandmother ordered the same books for herself and for her five-year-old granddaughter, and every Tuesday afternoon they Zoomed together, the grandmother reading aloud while her granddaughter turned over the pages of her copy. Musicians were quick to see the potential. On 18 May 2020 the Covenant House Choir's

Figure 10. Screengrab of the Covenant House Choir performing with Alex Newell during A Night Of Covenant House Stars, 18 May 2020. Used by permission of Covenant House International/Getty Images

annual gala benefit took place online, with the singers performing from their own homes (Figure 10). By August the Skagit Valley Chorale was meeting on Zoom. After the Glasgow Improvisers Orchestra migrated to Zoom the twenty-five or so local players were being joined by a further seventy from further afield, while Simon Lubkowski's Collective Virtual Choir attracted nearly 4,000 singers from sixty-six different countries to its daily rehearsals. For these participants musical togetherness survived physical separation, though of course it wasn't the same: some members of the Skagit

Valley Chorale dropped out on the grounds that the sense of community depends on 'a personal interaction ... that you can't get looking at the computer screen'.

Music took on new social forms in the pandemic, and here are two examples. The first is the synchronised listening parties that Tim Burgess, frontman of The Charlatans, had experimented with a few years earlier but that came into their own on 23 March 2020, the first day of the UK's first lockdown. Burgess announced the first party on Twitter, saying it would be based on The Charlatans' *Some Friendly* (1990), and explained what to do in another tweet: 'Stream or play the album in question and follow me and the relevant twitterer(s) and watch the tweets in real time. Ask questions/share memories etc using #timstwitterlisteningparty. Nowt complicated. That's it ;)'.[4] Everybody pressed go at the same time, and participants tweeted their thoughts as the music played. The following night it was Franz Ferdinand's eponymous album from 2004; the band's lead vocalist, Alex Kapranos, reminisced about the music while it played ('I still get a wee buzz when that slow down bit comes'), while bass guitarist Bob Hardie answered questions such as what they ate in the studio ('well done for getting down to the important stuff so quickly'). More than a thousand listening parties took place over the next two years. They are now archived on the web, and the first of a series of books based on them was published in 2021.[5]

My second example is the final episode from choral conductor Gareth Malone's BBC television series *The Choir: Singing for Britain*, first aired on 7 July 2020. Since 2006 Malone has created multiple series of *The Choir*, the purpose of which is to demonstrate the social benefits of choral singing. The formula is based on an environment (a town, a school, a prison) that lacks community, is socially deprived or otherwise failing. Malone puts together a choir of sometimes unenthusiastic locals, trains it, and against all the odds leads it to an astonishingly successful performance, after which participants speak emotionally of what they and their community have gained from the experience.

Obviously things had to work differently during the pandemic. The episode I mentioned focused on those who, through age or pre-existing conditions, were highly vulnerable to Covid and consequently shielded, along with their families or carers. Working remotely, we see Malone expertly draw out their experiences through conversation, and transform them into song – a song that is created both with and for the participants. The process releases a great deal of emotion among the participants, and the resulting songs are usually strongly personal. An exception is 'This is Just Another Storm', a song by fifteen-year-old Rae-Kwan: it is more universal in nature, more anthem-like, understanding Covid as just another natural disaster from which society will in time recover. The episode climaxes with a performance of it in the now familiar multiscreen format by the shielders and carers; they are joined by Malone's own virtual choir, the Great British Home Chorus (launched, like Tim Burgess's listening parties, on the first day of lockdown).[6]

How is it that music was able to create a sense of community, closeness, even intimacy when participants were physically separated from one another? To answer that you need to ask what it was that people were most missing – to which the answer is contact in the most literal sense. Music is created through touch. Look at Figure 11 and feel the harpist's finger pulling against the deflected strings, the way the strings cut into her flesh (male harpists are an endangered species), and the slightly rough texture of the wound strings; like guitarists, harpists can get callouses. Or think of the feel of a cellist's fingertip on the fingerboard, of an electric guitarist pushing and pulling on the whammy bar, of the semi-metaphorical idea of piano 'touch', or of

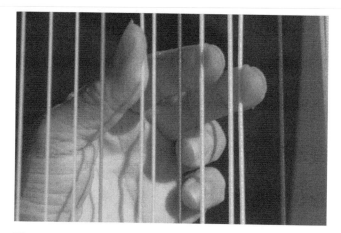

Figure 11. Harpist's hand. Photograph by Rama. Cropped reproduction under Creative Commons CC BY-SA 2.0 FR license (https://creativecommons.org/licenses/by-sa/2.0/fr/deed.en)

the title of François Couperin's *L'art de toucher le clavecin* (1716).

Equally we can be touched by music; that is, music touches us, just as partners, children, and friends do. Now put this together with what I said earlier, in connection with Daniel Stern, about how music embodies qualities of personhood. I talked about therapists' clients sometimes forming a relationship with music before they do so with the therapist, but the sense of relating to music as if it were some kind of virtual person can go further than that. Another therapy client described music as 'your soul-mate, your trusted secret friend who can empathize with you';[7] it's not just that you empathise with the music, it's that the music empathises with you, and so the relationship is somehow mutual. I am reminded of the 'social robots' now in use in Japan, which are designed specifically to offer care and personal companionship to the elderly; people become attached to them, for example knitting them bonnets.[8] After all, what can be more human than caring?

'For many people', say neuroscientists Francis McGlone and Susannah Walker, 'the thing they've missed most during the pandemic is being able to hug loved ones'. The hard, flat screen of a computer is no substitute for the sensuously – or sensually – yielding feel of warm, living skin on skin; touch, McGlone and Walker continue, is 'an extremely important sense that allows us not only to physically explore the world around us, but also to communicate with others by creating and maintaining social bonds'.[9] Another neuroscientist, David Linden, describes interpersonal touch as 'a crucial form of social glue' that connects people and fosters 'emotions of gratitude, sympathy, and trust' ; a hug doesn't just feel good, it does you good.[10] Linden also emphasises the crucial role of social touch in development, and of course infant–carer communication is just as much a relationship of touch as it is of sound. He speaks of 'the brain's specialized centers for emotional touch' as 'crossroads where sensation and expectation collide, allowing for powerful effects of life history, culture, and context' – the same words I used of music a few pages back (only that time I didn't attribute them to Linden). Finally he entitles his first chapter 'The Skin Is a Social Organ' – and so is the ear.

Then again, musicologist Luis-Manuel Garcia Mispirita, writing of electronic dance music (EDM), emphasises how – especially at low frequencies – vibrations are perceived equally as sound, touch, and affect. (A *New York Times* newsletter contributor wrote of an organ concert, the first live music he had heard in two years, 'there is nothing like the feeling in your chest when the organist plays the low notes. Sorry, YouTube, it just isn't the same online.') Garcia speaks of how EDM uses sounds that emanate from the human body – or at least that sound as if they do – to induce effects of fleshy materiality, stressing that these are effects of direct perception rather than working through symbolic or structural cues. Finally he suggests that the ill-defined aspect of music that we call texture should be thought of not as something specifically musical or even sonic, but rather as 'an amodal phenomenon . . . that extends beyond the remit of any particular sense organ'.[11]

From here it is no great stretch to suggest that we might think of music as sonic touching, or touch as haptic musicking – or, in Roshanak Kheshti's formulation, that sound and touch 'double in on one another to construct an imaginary site of contact with *other* bodies'.[12] By that I understand not just contact with imaginary bodies but imagined contact with real bodies.

But I can also explain what I am talking about more straightforwardly. In a newspaper article published a few months into the pandemic, journalist Amy Fleming wrote about entrainment: 'when two people walk together', she said, 'they unconsciously fall into step', and she continued, 'the more in sync we are, the deeper our social connection, so walking in step is pretty much a physically distanced hug'.[13] In the same way, when music empathises with you, when it touches you, envelops you, that too is pretty much a physically distanced hug. It is intimacy, but a contactless, Covid-secure form of intimacy. And perhaps the most poignant example of this to emerge from the pandemic is the balcony music that regularly took place in Italian towns during the first and cruellest European surge of Covid-19. Residents came out onto their balconies to sing or play to their neighbours, using music to tell one another that even in lockdown you are not alone (Figure 12).

Figure 12. Italian balcony music during lockdown in San Salvario, Turin, March 2020. Photograph by Nicolò Campo/LightRocket. Getty Images

I think in particular of Paola Agnelli and Michele D'Alpaos, who were respectively living on the sixth and seventh floors of their blocks on opposite sides of the road in Verona (Verona of all places!). On 17 March 2020 Paola's sister Lisa was playing Queen's 'We Are the Champions' on her violin when the latter-day Romeo and Juliet simultaneously stepped out onto their respective balconies. Their eyes locked and it was love at first sight. They communicated through balcony-to-balcony messages – one day Michele hung out a sheet with PAOLA written on it – and then he tracked her down on

Instagram. In May, after lockdown had lifted, they had their first kiss. And this drama turned out better than Shakespeare's: by September it was reported that they were planning their wedding.[14]

Don't you love a happy ending?

Further Reading

A very different – but complementary – take on why music matters is offered by sociologist David Hesmondhalgh's book of that name. A longer book than mine, it focuses on the role music plays in social life and how we might think more adequately about it: David Hesmondhalgh, *Why Music Matters* (Wiley Blackwell, 2013).

Music, health, and wellbeing

Pioneering studies of social uses of Western music include Ruth Finnegan's *The Hidden Musicians: Music-Making in an English Town* (Cambridge University Press, 1989) and Tia DeNora's *Music in Everyday Life* (Cambridge University Press, 2000); Thomas Turino provides an ethnomusicological perspective in *Music as Social Life: The Politics of Participation* (University of Chicago Press, 2008). A standard introduction to music in the community is Lee Higgins, *Community Music: In Theory and in Practice* (Oxford University Press, 2000),

Further Reading

while in *A Different Voice, a Different Song: Reclaiming Community Through the Natural Voice and World Song* (Oxford University Press, 2014) Caroline Bithell focuses on a specific area within community music. Gary Ansdell provides an approachable and inspiring introduction to music therapy and the larger area of music and wellbeing in *How Music Helps in Music Therapy and Everyday Life* (Routledge, 2014).

Socialities of musicking

I said that academic interest in the socialities of musicking seems to be surging. A wide-ranging collection of cutting-edge work, employing a variety of mainly empirical methods, is Renee Timmers, Freya Bayles, and Helena Daffern (eds), *Together in Music: Coordination, Expression, Participation* (Oxford University Press, 2021); the book ranges from micro to macro dimensions of the subject and includes a section on health and wellness musicking. I also discuss the topic from a more specifically musicological perspective in *Music, Encounter, Togetherness* (see below).

Music and race

Philip Ewell's 'Music theory and the white racial frame', which I discussed in the section '2020 and After', is published in *Music Theory Online* 26/2 (2020); Matthew Morrison's article 'Race, Blacksound, and the (re)making of musicological discourse' is an example of how new racial thinking is changing historical musicology (*Journal*

Further Reading

of the American Musicological Society 72/3 (2019), pp. 781–823). *White Fragility*, by Robin DiAngelo (Allen Lane, 2019), is an introduction to the basic principles of critical race theory aimed primarily at white readers; Richard Delgado and Jean Stefancic offer a more formal introduction to CRT in *Critical Race Theory: An Introduction* (New York University Press, 2017). Otegha Uwagba's *Whites: On Race and Other Falsehoods* (Fourth Estate, 2020) is a succinct account of Black experience in Britain in the wake of the George Floyd killing.

Music and politics

D. R. M. Irving's *The Making of 'European Music' in the Long Eighteenth Century* (Oxford University Press, forthcoming) is a study of how the very ideas of European and Western music were associated with colonialism and such imperialist values as exceptionalism and universalism. A general introduction to the relationship between music and politics is provided by James Garratt in *Music and Politics: A Critical Introduction* (Cambridge University Press, 2018), while a collection edited by Robert Adlington and Esteban Buch called *Finding Democracy in Music* (Routledge, 2021) explores ways in which music can embody specifically democratic values.

Music and ethics

Jeff Warren explores music and human relationship from an ethical perspective in *Music and Ethical Responsibility*

Further Reading

(Cambridge University Press, 2014); William Cheng asks what happens when commitments to music and to social justice collide in *Loving Music Till it Hurts* (Oxford University Press, 2019).

Finally

Readers after a concise and accessible introduction to music, placing Western classical music and thinking about it in a wider musical context, might try my *Music: A Very Short Introduction* (second edition, Oxford University Press, 2021). The approach to music, performance, and interpersonal relationship I have taken in the present book is explored in much greater detail, with further references, in *Music, Encounter, Togetherness* (Oxford University Press, forthcoming).

Notes

Music for Good or Ill

1 *The Importance of Music: A National Plan for Music Education*, Department of Education, 2011.
2 Colin Harris, 'Behold: The dying art of the peripatetic music teacher', *TES Magazine*, 30 March 2020.
3 Tia DeNora, *Music Asylums: Wellbeing through Music in Everyday Life*, Routledge, 2016.
4 Eric Clarke, Tia DeNora, and Jonna Vuoskoski, 'Music, empathy and cultural understanding', *Physics of Life Reviews* 15, 2015, p. 77.
5 'Daniel Barenboim and Edward Said upon receiving the "Principe de Asturias" Prize', 2002.
6 Geoffrey Baker, *Rethinking Social Action through Music: The Search for Coexistence and Citizenship in Medellín's Music Schools*, Open Book Publishers, 2021, p. 21.
7 Joe Stroud, 'The importance of music to Anders Behring Breivik', *Journal of Terrorism Research* 4/1, 2013, p. 10.

8 Suzanne Cusick, '"You are in a place that is out of the world . . .": Music in the detention camps of the "Global War on Terror"', *Journal of the Society for American Music* 2/1, 2008, p. 4.

Ideology in Disguise

1 Daniel Leech-Wilkinson, *Challenging Performance: Classical Music Performance Norms and How to Escape Them*, version 2.14, chapter 3.1, at https:// challengingperformance.com/the-book (All websites accessible on 31 October 2022 unless otherwise stated.)

2 Robin DiAngelo, *White Fragility*, Allen Lane, 2019, p. 57.

3 DiAngelo, *White Fragility*, p. 52.

4 As of this writing the commercial is at https://www. youtube.com/watch?v=Z_0Takot9eM.

5 James Garratt, *Music and Politics*, Cambridge University Press, 2018, p. 21.

6 Beverley Nichols, *Verdict on India*, Jonathan Cape, 1944, p. 135.

Music, Race, Empire

1 Matthew Morrison, 'Race, Blacksound, and the (re) making of musicological discourse', *Journal of the American Musicological Society* 72/3, 2019, p. 790.

2 William Berwick Sayers, *Samuel Coleridge-Taylor – Musician: His Life and Letters*, Cassell, 1915, p. 71.

3 Kira Thurman, 'Performing Lieder, hearing race:

Debating Blackness, whiteness, and German identity in interwar Central Europe', *Journal of the American Musicological Society* 72/3, 2019, p. 849.

4 Accessible at https://www.bbc.co.uk/programmes/p00941vr.

5 Quoted in Mari Yoshihara, *Musicians from a Different Shore: Asians and Asian Americans in Classical Music*, Temple University Press, 2007, p. 188.

6 Quoted in Freya de Mink, *Musical Prodigies: Past, Present, and Future Perspectives on Exceptional Performance and Creativity*, MMus dissertation, Utrecht University, 2013, p. 56.

7 Anthony Sheppard, 'The persistence of Orientalism in the postmodern operas of Adams and Sellars', in Joshua Walden (ed.), *Representation in Western Music*, Cambridge University Press, 2013.

8 D. R. M. Irving, *The Making of 'European Music' in the Long Eighteenth Century*, Oxford University Press, forthcoming.

9 Jonathan Rutherford, *Identity: Community, Culture, Difference*, Lawrence and Wishart, 1990, p. 208.

10 Katherine Schofield, 'Sophia Plowden, Khanum Jan, and their Hindustani airs' (blogpost) https://zenodo.org/record/1445769#.XS2txZNKhE5. I have written on this at length in *Music, Encounter, Togetherness*, Oxford University Press, forthcoming.

11 'Songs are dangerous little bombs of truth: Nick Cave and Sean O'Hagan – An exclusive book extract', *Guardian*, 11 September 2022.

2020 and After

1 Otegha Uwagba, *Whites: On Race and Other Falsehoods*, Fourth Estate, 2020, p. 10.

2 E.g. Peter McMurray, 'Witnessing race in the new digital cinema', in Nicholas Cook, Monique Ingalls and David Trippett (eds), *The Cambridge Companion to Music in Digital Culture*, Cambridge University Press, 2019.

3 Philip Bohlman and Federico Celestini, 'Editorial: Reckoning with musicology's past and present', *Acta Musicologica* 92/2, 2020.

4 Carl Schachter, 'Elephants, crocodiles, and Beethoven: Schenker's politics and the pedagogy of Schenkerian analysis', *Theory and Practice* 26, 2001, p. 13.

5 Heinrich Schenker, *Der Tonwille: Pamphlets in Witness of the Immutable Laws of Music: Issues 1–5 (1921–1923)*, ed. William Drabkin, trans. Ian Bent et al., Oxford University Press, 2004, p. 15. African troops in the Saarland and the adjacent Rhineland were a focus of racist attack, as illustrated by a post-card from around 1920 showing a white rape victim and the slogan 'The "black shame": How long must this go on?', https://blackcentraleurope.com/sources/1914-1945/the-black-shame-how-long-must-this-go-on-ca-1920.

6 Heinrich Schenker, *Beethoven's Last Five Piano Sonatas: An Edition with Elucidations, Vol. 3: Piano Sonata in C minor, Op 111*, trans. John Rothgeb, Oxford University Press, 2015. The quote is in

the Literature section on the Companion website, p. 21.

7 Heinrich Schenker, diary entry for 13 October 1915, translated by William Drabkin (Schenker Documents Online, https://schenkerdocumentsonline.org/docu ments/diaries/OJ-01-19_1915-10/r0013.html). Thanks to Bill for telling me about this.

8 Ewell, 'Music theory and the white racial frame', *Music Theory Online* 26/2, 2020, paras 4.5.4, 4.2.6.

9 Ewell, 'Music theory and the white racial frame', para 4.5.5.

10 Shortly after I wrote this a controversy erupted when the UK Quality Assurance Agency stipulated that mathematics curricula 'should present a multicul- tural and decolonised view' of the field, also warning that 'divisions and hierarchies of colonial value are replicated and reinforced' within computing stud- ies. Eleanor Harding, 'Universities are ordered to go woke', *Mail Online*, 15 November 2022.

11 'Symposium on Philip Ewell's SMT 2019 Plenary paper, "Music theory's white racial frame"', *Journal of Schenkerian Studies* 12, 2019.

12 Accessible at https://www.facebook.com/breadcam bridge/posts/d41d8cd9/2690221287876849.

13 As documented by Ewell in 'Erasing colorasure in American music theory, and confronting demons from our past', *Bibliolore* (RILM blog), 25 March 2021.

14 Steven Rings, 'Music's stubborn enchantments (and music theory's)', *Music Theory Online* 24/1, 2018, abstract.

15 Bryan Parkhurst, '*Composing Capital: Classical Music in the Neoliberal Era.* By Marianna Ritchey' [review], *Music Theory Spectrum* 42/2, 2020. He is quoting Rings.

16 Ewell himself advocated this in answer to a question following his talk 'How we got here, where to next: Examining assimilationism in American music studies' (CUNY Graduate Center, 4 December 2020; video no longer accessible on the web). Like me, Ewell prefers the term 'music studies'.

17 Uwagba, *Whites*, p. 23.

18 Accessible at https://zhuanlan.zhihu.com/p/2732012 92. Posted on the Jiscmail Musicology-All list, 2 November 2020. The authors are listed as Monica Moreno Figueroa, Gayle Murchison, Shzr Ee Tan, and Hettie Malcolmson.

Music and Asocial Individualism

1 DiAngelo, *White Fragility*, pp. 20–1.

2 For a highly practical description of colourblindness in music teaching see Catherine Bradley, 'Hidden in plain sight: Race and racism in music education', in Cathy Benedict et al. (eds), *The Oxford Handbook of Social Justice in Music Education*, Oxford University Press, 2015.

3 Elizabeth Mackinlay, 'Decolonization and applied ethnomusicology: "Storying" the personal-political-possible in our work', in Svanibor Pettan and Jeff Todd Titon (eds), *The Oxford Handbook of Applied Ethnomusicology*, Oxford University Press, 2015.

4 Published as Thomas Carlyle, *On Heroes, Hero-Worship and the Heroic in History*, Chapman and Hall, 1841.

5 Boris Johnson, *The Churchill Factor: How One Man Made History*, Hodder & Stoughton, 2014, p. 45.

6 Timothy Taylor, *Music and Capitalism*, University of Chicago Press, 2015, p. 32.

7 Jonathan Freedland, 'The new age of Ayn Rand: How she won over Trump and Silicon Valley', *Guardian*, 10 April 2017.

8 Kwasi Kwarteng, Priti Patel, Dominic Raab, Chris Skidmore and Elizabeth Truss, *Britannia Unchained: Global Lessons for Growth and Prosperity*, Palgrave Macmillan, 2012.

9 Jon Cruddas, 'Britannia Unchained: Global Lessons for Growth and Prosperity – review', *Guardian*, 27 September 2012.

10 James Dale Davidson and Lord William Rees-Mogg, *The Sovereign Individual: Mastering the Transition to the Information Age*, Touchstone, 1999, pp. 17–18.

11 Crawford Brough Macpherson, *The Political Theory of Possessive Individualism: From Hobbes to Locke*, Clarendon Press, 1962, p. 3.

12 Heather Stewart, 'Boris Johnson yet again avoids paying the price for his cavalier attitude', *Guardian*, 8 July 2021.

13 David Runciman, 'The crisis of British democracy', *Juncture* 20/3, 2013, p. 170.

14 Wendy Brown, *Undoing the Demos: Neoliberalism's Stealth Revolution*, Zone Books, 2015, p. 179.

15 Heinrich Schenker, *Harmony*, ed. Oswald Jonas,

trans. Elisabeth Mann Borgese, University of Chicago Press, 1954, pp. 60–1.

16 Quoted in Michel Eltchaninoff, 'What's going on inside Putin's mind? His own words give us a disturbing clue', *Guardian*, 25 February 2022.

17 Peter Pomerantsev, 'Vladimir Putin: What's going on inside his head?', *Guardian*, 26 February 2022.

Music, Nostalgia, Delusion

1 Catherine Loveday, Amy Woy, and Martin Conway, 'The self-defining period in autobiographical memory: Evidence from a long-running radio show', *Quarterly Journal of Experimental Psychology* 73/11, 2020.

2 Daniel Grimley, *Delius and the Sound of Place*, Cambridge University Press, 2018, p. 49.

3 Dave Harker, *Fakesong: The Manufacture of British 'Folksong', 1700 to the Present Day*, Open University Press, 1985.

4 Cecil Sharp, *English Folk-Song: Some Conclusions*, Simpkin and Co, 1907, p. 136.

5 Paul Revoir, 'Castaway? Patriotic public choose Vaughan Williams for their top Desert Island Disc', *Mail Online*, 13 June 2011.

6 Mike Finn, 'Post-war fantasies and Brexit: The delusional view of Britain's place in the world', LSE British Politics and Policy blog (2016).

7 Mary O'Connor, 'Ukraine war: Boris Johnson sparks fury after comparison to Brexit', *Guardian*, 20 March 2022.

8 Henrietta Marshall, *Our Island Story: A History of England for Boys and Girls*, Thomas Nelson, [1905], p. 340.

9 Speech at Conservative Party Conference, 5 October 2010, formerly at https://conservative-speeches.sayit.mysociety.org/speech/601441.

10 Quoted in Ben Wellings, 'Our Island Story: England, Europe and the Anglosphere alternative', *Political Studies Review* 14/3, 2016.

11 Penelope Lively, *Oleander, Jacaranda: A Childhood Perceived*, Penguin Books, 1995, pp. 18–19.

12 J. R. R. Tolkien, *The Lord of the Rings*, HarperCollins ebooks, 2020, p. 578.

13 William Davies, *This is Not Normal: The Collapse of Liberal Britain*, Verso, 2020, p. 169.

14 Quoted in Ron Suskind, 'Faith, certainty and the presidency of George W. Bush', *New York Times*, 17 October 2004.

15 Davies, *This is Not Normal*, p. 144.

16 William Gibson, *Neuromancer*, Berkley Publishing Group, 1989, p. 128.

17 Rafael Behr, 'The "Boris effect" is a symptom of Britain's decaying political system', *Guardian*, 28 July 2021.

Music and Administered Society

1 Leech-Wilkinson, *Challenging Performance*, chapter 9.2.

2 Lydia Goehr, *The Imaginary Museum of Musical Works: An Essay in the Philosophy of Music*, Oxford University Press, 1994.

3 Tim Ingold, *The Life of Lines*, Routledge, 2015, p. 105.

4 Ben Sidran, *Black Talk: How the Music of Black America Created a Radical Alternative to the Values of Western Literary Tradition*, Payback Press, 1995, p. 6.

5 Quoted in Benjamin Givan, 'How democratic is jazz?', in Robert Adlington and Esteban Buch (eds), *Finding Democracy in Music*, Routledge, 2021, p. 61.

6 Dean Rowan, 'Modes and manifestations of improvisation in urban planning, design, and theory', *Critical Studies in Improvisation* 1/1, 2004, p. 21.

7 Robert Adlington and Esteban Buch, 'Introduction: Looking for democracy in music and elsewhere', in Adlington and Buch (eds), *Finding Democracy in Music*, p. 7.

8 Anna Bull, *Class, Control, and Classical Music*, Oxford University Press, 2019.

9 Quoted in Garratt, *Music and Politics*, pp. 175–6.

10 Lawrence Gushee, 'The improvisation of Louis Armstrong', in Bruno Nettl with Melinda Russell (eds), *In the Course of Performance: Studies in the World of Musical Improvisation*, University of Chicago Press, 1998.

11 Christopher Hasty, 'Learning in time', *Visions of Research in Music Education* 20, 2012.

12 Rob Shields, *The Virtual*, Routledge, 2003, p. 134.

13 Stephen Cottrell, *Professional Music-Making in London: Ethnography and Experience*, Routledge, 2004, pp. 105–7.

Musical Togetherness

1 Quoted in Joshua Needelman, 'How LeVar Burton (and others) helped us get through the pandemic', *New York Times*, 26 September 2022.

2 Quoted in Matthew Laube, *Music and Confession in Heidelberg, 1556–1618*, PhD dissertation, Royal Holloway, University of London, 2014, p. 80.

3 Stephen Mithen, *The Singing Neanderthals: The Origins of Music, Language, Mind and Body*, Weidenfeld and Nicolson, 2005, pp. 208–9.

4 Ian Cross, 'Music and communication in music psychology', *Music Psychology* 42/6, 2014.

5 James Naughtie, 'John le Carré: "Politicians love chaos – it gives them authority"', BBC News website, 14 October 2019.

6 Nancy Love, *Trendy Fascism: White Power Music and the Future of Democracy*, State University of New York Press, 2016, p. 6.

7 Stephen Malloch and Colwyn Trevarthen (eds), *Communicative Musicality: Exploring the Basis of Human Companionship*, Oxford University Press, 2008.

8 Daniel Stern, *The Present Moment in Psychotherapy and Everyday Life*, Norton, 2004, p. 26.

9 Daniel Stern, *Forms of Vitality: Exploring Dynamic Experience in Psychology, the Arts, Psychotherapy, and Development*, Oxford University Press, 2010, p. 6.

10 Alfred Schutz, 'Making music together: A study in social relationship', *Social Research* 18/1, 1951, p. 94.

11 Tim Ingold and Elizabeth Hallam, 'Creativity and cultural improvisation: An introduction', in Elizabeth Hallam and Tim Ingold (eds), *Creativity and Cultural Improvisation*, Berg, 2007, p. 6.

12 Keith Sawyer, *Group Creativity: Music, Theater, Collaboration*, Lawrence Erlbaum, 2003, pp. 86–93.

Music, Covid, Ethics

1 Charles Taylor, *The Malaise of Modernity*, Anansi, 1991.

2 Tyler Stovall, *White Freedom: The Racial History of an Idea*, Princeton University Press, 2021.

3 Linda Geddes, 'UK scientists caution that lifting of Covid rules is like building "variant factories"', *Guardian*, 4 July 2021.

4 Michael Savage and Robin McKie, 'Tory MPs warn Boris Johnson's rivals to oppose tougher Covid new year rules', *Guardian*, 26 December 2021.

5 Aditya Chakrabortty, 'After Covid, the climate crisis will be the next thing the right says we "just have to live with"', *Guardian*, 22 July 2021.

6 Jonathan Sumption, '"This is how freedom dies": The folly of Britain's coercive Covid strategy', *Spectator*, 28 October 2020.

7 Stephen Reicher, 'With Covid cases soaring and the NHS in trouble, here's how to end the culture war on face masks', *Guardian*, 5 January 2023.

8 Charles Taylor, *Sources of the Self: The Making of Modern Identity*, Cambridge University Press, 1992, pp. 111–12.

9 John Bailey, *Guardian*, 11 March 2022.

10 'Ahead of hearing, Committee releases memo showing fossil fuel industry is misleading the public about commitment to reduce emissions' (press release), House Committee on Oversight and Reform, 14 September 2022.

11 Matthew Taylor, 'More than 50 Just Stop Oil protesters in UK sent to jail on one day', *Guardian*, 14 September 2022.

12 Matthew Taylor, '"Grotesque greed": Immoral fossil fuel profits must be taxed, says UN chief', *Guardian*, 3 August 2022.

13 David Blum, *The Art of Quartet Playing: The Guarneri Quartet in Conversation with David Blum*, Cornell University Press, 1986, p. 20; Arnold Steinhardt, *Indivisible by Four: A String Quartet in Pursuit of Harmony*, Farrar, Straus and Giroux, 2000, pp. 301–6. Steinhardt offers an autoethnographic account of the Quartet performing Schubert's 'Death and the Maiden'. At one point, for instance, Steinhardt and the cellist David Soyer 'trade off quarter notes slurred into chords. We are angry gods hurling thunderbolts across the sky at one another. But David's thunderbolts are different every night, and since he throws first I must be prepared for anything' (p. 304).

14 Davies, *This is Not Normal*, p. 121.

15 James Saunders, 'Group behaviours as music', in Renee Timmers, Freya Bayles, and Helena Daffern (eds), *Together in Music: Cooordination, Expression, Participation*, Oxford University Press, 2021, p. 18.

16 Ehud Bodner and Avi Gilboa, 'On the power of music

to affect intergroup relations', *Musicae Scientiae* 13/1, 2009.

17 Marianna Ritchey, *Composing Capital: Classical Music in the Neoliberal Era*, University of Chicago Press, 2019, p. 4.

18 Uwagba, *Whites*, p. 84.

19 Stephanie Brobbey, 'I help rich people tackle inequality. Here's how the cost-of-living crisis could be fixed', *Guardian*, 6 July 2022.

20 Rebecca Solnit, 'Why are US rightwingers so angry? Because they know social change is coming', *Guardian*, 20 December 2021.

Pandemic Intimacy

1 *The Heart of the School is Missing: Music Education in the Covid-19 Crisis*, Incorporated Society of Musicians, December 2020.

2 Kim Tingley, 'All together now', *New York Times Magazine*, April 2021. However, a research study published while this book was in proof indicates that the Skagit rehearsal was not, as thought, a superspreader event based on a single infected individual; it appears that many of those who fell ill had been infected prior to the rehearsal. That would mean the UK government's 18-month ban on amateur choral singing was unnecessary. (Colin Axon, Robert Dingwall, Sam Evans and Jackie Cassel, 'The Skagit County choir COVID-19 outbreak – have we got it wrong?', *Public Health* 214, 2023, pp. 85–90.)

3 In J. G. Ballard, *The Complete Short Stories: Volume 2*, Flamingo, 2001, pp. 946–52. Ballard imagines a world where people rarely if ever meet in the flesh and instead communicate via television; a family's attempt to come physically together ends in disaster.

4 https://twitter.com/tim_burgess/status/1243311699 941261313, 26 March 2020.

5 Tim Burgess, *The Listening Party: Artists, Bands and Fans Reflect on 100 Favorite Albums*, Penguin Random House, 2021. The listening party website is at https://timstwitterlisteningparty.com (select 'Replay' for the web archive).

6 At publication time this episode is not available on the internet, but there is a clip that includes Rae-Kwan's song at https://www.youtube.com/watch?v= gw3loTdWXw0.

7 Anemieke Van den Tol and Jane Edwards, 'Exploring a rationale for choosing to listen to sad music when feeling sad', *Psychology of Music* 41/1, 2011, p. 453.

8 Noreena Hertz in 'Rethink population: What Japan can teach us', BBC Radio 4, 6 January 2022, https:// www.bbc.co.uk/sounds/play/m00132tj.

9 Francis McGlone and Susannah Walker, 'Four ways hugs are good for your health', *Greater Good Magazine*, 22 June 2021.

10 David Linden, *Touch: The Science of the Sense that Makes Us Human*, Penguin Books, 2016, p. 5.

11 Luis-Manuel Garcia Mispirita, 'Beats, flesh, and grain: Sonic tactility and affect in electronic dance music', *Sound Studies* 1/1, 2015, p. 72.

12 Roshanak Kheshti, 'Touching listening: The aural

imaginary in the world music culture industry', *American Quarterly* 63/3, 2011, p. 712.

13 Amy Fleming, 'Walk this way! How to optimise your stride and focus your mind to get the most from your daily stroll', *Guardian*, 28 May 2020.

14 See e.g. Alaa Elassar, 'An Italian couple who met on their balconies during quarantine are now engaged in the same city where "Romeo and Juliet" was set', CNN, 4 October 2020.

Index

Index

Index

Index

Index

Index